BARRON'S

Grammar
Third Edition

Vincent F. Hopper
Cedric Gale
Formerly of New York University

Ronald C. Foote
Formerly of California State University, Long Beach

Revised by
Benjamin W. Griffith
Formerly of State University of West Georgia

Barron's Educational Series, Inc.

©Copyright 1997 by Barron's Educational Series, Inc.
Prior editions © Copyright 1990 and 1984 by Barron's
Educational Series, Inc.
Formerly published as *Essentials of English* and as
Essentials of Effective Writing.

All inquiries should be addressed to:
Barron's Educational Series, Inc.
250 Wireless Boulevard
Hauppauge, New York 11788

Library of Congress Catalog Card No. 96-54635

International Standard Book No. 0-8120-9815-3

Library of Congress Cataloging-in-Publication Data
Hopper, Vincent Foster, 1906-
    A pocket guide to correct grammar / Vincent F. Hopper,
Cedric Gale, Ronald C. Foote. — 3rd ed. / revised by Benjamin
W. Griffith.
        p.   cm.
    At head of title: Barron's.
    Includes index.
    ISBN 0-8120-9815-3
    1. English language—Grammar. 2. English language—
Rhetoric. I. Gale, Cedric, 1905- . II. Foote, Ronald C.
III. Griffith, Benjamin W. IV. Title.
PE1112.H65   1997
428.2—dc21   96-54635
                                                        CIP

PRINTED IN THE UNITED STATES OF AMERICA
9 8 7 6 5 4 3 2

CONTENTS

PREFACE

A Pocket Guide to Correct Grammar is designed to be a handy reference tool for everyone who aspires to write and speak correct English. In this informal age some might ask, "Who worries about *correct* English?" The answer is that most success-oriented Americans are grammar-conscious Americans. Like it or not, many people judge us by our skill in using English correctly.

This pocket guide is based on traditional grammar usage. It is organized along conventional lines, with an easy-to-use table of contents and index. Before beginning to use the guide extensively, get acquainted with the entire book by scanning it from beginning to end. There is a great deal of information on a relatively few pages. We hope that it is clear, readily usable information and that the examples given can help you gain a thorough grasp of the technical points of grammar. In the final analysis, however, only practice and repetition can lead to a complete understanding.

Chapter 1
The Word

Just as expert carpenters must be thoroughly acquainted with the tools of their craft and as painters must have expert knowledge of colors, so good writers must have a thorough understanding of the basic material with which they work: **words.** Thoughts and utterances, both simple and complex, require words of several kinds— for example, naming words, asserting words, connecting words, descriptive words. One of the first steps to effective writing is, therefore, a knowledge of the properties and functions of the different kinds of words. This knowledge involves what a word looks like, where it appears, and what it does within its context.

THE NOUN

The noun is a naming word. It is used to identify people, places, objects, ideas, emotions—in short, anything that can be named: *John, Chicago, committee, amplification, table, hatred, baseball.*

Recognition of Nouns

Nouns can be recognized by their form and their position in the sentence as well as by their naming function. Below are some of the things to look for when you are trying to identify the nouns in a sentence. (The principles listed here are discussed in greater detail in other sections of the book.)

➤ Most nouns can follow the word *the* or other determiners such as

> *my, a, this: a truth, his moves, this infatuation.*

➤ All nouns can occur before and after verbs:

> *His* **moves** *dazzled the* **spectators. Faith** *moves* **mountains.**

➤ All nouns can follow relationship words called prepositions:

> *before winter, after Christmas, in his adversity.*

➤ Most nouns can take an s or an *es* at the end of the word to express the idea of more than one:

> *soup, soups; church, churches; debate, debates.*

➤ Some nouns can take an apostrophe and an s or an apostrophe by itself to express belonging:

> *the* **boy's** *bicycle; the* **boys'** *room.*

➤ Some nouns can start with a capital letter to indicate the name or the title of some specific thing or person:

> *Wilson High School, Armando, America, September, Surgeon General.*

➤ Some nouns have endings such as *-ness, -tion, -ity,* which indicates that the word is a noun:

> *reasonableness, situation, adversity.*

Proper and Common Nouns

The name or title of an individual, of a person, place, or thing is usually expressed by a proper noun or nouns. They are always capitalized. When these nouns do *not* refer to the name of a person or thing, they are common nouns and are *not* capitalized. Compare:

> I will ask *Mother.*
> Yesterday she became a *mother.*

> I think that *Crescent City* is in Alberta.
> The *city* lay on a crescent in the river.

> He settled in the *West.*
> He drove *west* for ten miles.

Among other things, proper nouns name people, continents, countries, provinces, states, counties, parishes, geographic regions, days of the week, months of the year, holidays, festivals (but not seasons):

> *Christmas, winter, December, Friday, Alberta, the Netherlands, Judge Hernandez.*

Singular and Plural Nouns

Most nouns can be singular or plural in form. The usual plural form adds *s* or *es* to the end of the word: *sigh, sighs; fox, foxes; category, categories; calf, calves.* Note that the *y* and the *f* change before a plural ending. **Trys* and **skys* are incorrect forms. There is less consistency with the *f* forms. *Hoofs* is possible; **rooves* is not. It is advisable to have a dictionary at hand when dealing with some plurals.

Some nouns have irregular plural forms: *child, children; goose, geese; sheep, sheep.* Some nouns borrowed from other languages keep their original plural forms: *datum, data; cherub, cherubim; crisis, crises.* Other foreign words use either an Anglicized

---

*Throughout the text, an asterisk will be used to indicate an incorrect form in Standard American English.

plural or the foreign plural: *appendix, appendixes/ appendices; curriculum, curriculums/curricula; formula, formulas/formulae.* An up-to-date dictionary is helpful in determining the correct foreign plurals.

Some nouns can normally occur in the singular form only: *much dust*, but not **much dusts; more courage*, but not **more courages; less fun*, but not **less funs.* These nouns are called mass nouns or non-countable nouns. Some determiners such as *much* and *less* should be used only with non-countable nouns although recently there has been a tendency among educated speakers to use **less people* (*people* is a countable noun) rather than *fewer people.*

A few non-countable nouns can appear in the plural form if the idea of a difference of kind is stressed. *There are some new instant coffees on the market. Several wheats grow in Australia.*

The Possessive Case of Nouns

The possessive case of nouns is formed by adding an apostrophe and an *s* to words that do not end with an *s* or a *z* sound: *the boy's room, the children's school;* and by adding only the apostrophe to words which do end with an *s* or a *z* sound: *the boys' room, Dickens' novel.* If, however, the word ending in *s* or *z* is a proper noun with only one syllable, an apostrophe and an *s* are added to the word: *Keats's sonnets, Santa Claus's reindeer.*

NOTE: Some classical names and other names that would be awkward to pronounce with an added apostrophe and *s* use only the apostrophe: *Xerxes' chariot, Moses' tablets.*

Care must be taken in forming the possessive form of nouns ending with *y* because although the singular and plural forms sound the same way, they are spelled differently.

> the baby's cry
> (one baby's cry)
>
> the babies' murmurings
> (the murmurings of several babies)

When possession is shared by two or more nouns, this fact is indicated by using the possessive case for the last noun in the series: *Jose, Fred, and Edward's canoe.*

When two nouns refer to the same person, the second noun is in the possessive case.

> *the mother of the bride's yellow dress*
> (The bride probably wore white. If the phrase sounds awkward, the use of two possessives does not improve it much: *the bride's mother's yellow dress.*)
> Better: *The yellow dress of the bride's mother.*

The Apostrophe Possessive and the "OF" Possessive

Inanimate things do not normally "possess" anything. The possessive form using the preposition *of* is used to express an arrangement or part of inanimate things.

> piles of coats **NOT** *coats' piles
> the edge of the chisel **NOT** *the chisel's edge

However, writers have long made exception to this rule: *a day's work, a dollar's worth, the ship's compass.* More and more inanimate things are taking the apostrophe form of the possessive: *the razor's edge, the book's success, education's failure.* Obviously, no clear rule can be stated where *the razor's edge* is approved of and *the chisel's edge* is not.

Functions of Nouns

The noun can perform a variety of functions. The functions listed here are discussed in greater detail in other sections of the book.

➤ *The noun can work as the subject, object, or comple-*
ment of a finite verb or verbal.

> Being a recent *arrival*
> (complement of the verbal *being*)
>
> from Puerto Rico, *Margarita*
> (subject of the verb was)
>
> was proud that she could speak *Spanish*
> (object of the verb *speak*)
>
> as well as English.

➤ *The noun can work as the object of a preposition.*

> Margarita, who came from *Puerto Rico,*
> (object of the preposition *from*)
>
> spoke excellent Spanish in her *home*
> (object of the preposition *in*)
>
> and good English at *school.*
> (object of the preposition *at*)

➤ *The noun can work after another noun as a modifier or*
an appositive, as it is also called.

> my brother *Charles*
> his problem, a damaged *retina*

➤ *The noun can work before another noun as a modifier.*

> a *problem* child   a *noun* clause   a *bottle* opener

➤ *The noun can work as a modifier of an adjective or a verb.*

> They were *battle* weary.
> (modifier of the adjective *weary*)

> They arrived *yesterday.*
> (modifier of the verb *arrived*)

➤ *The noun in the possessive case can work as a determiner introducing another noun.*

> the *bride's mother*
> (*The bride's* introduces *mother.* The article *the* belongs to *bride's,* not to *mother.*)

THE PRONOUN

Although a pronoun often takes the place of a noun in a sentence, the pronoun sometimes lacks specific meaning. Indefinite pronouns like *anyone, something, somebody* mean only that unspecified people or things are being referred to.

When pronouns replace other words, they carry the meaning of the replaced words. The replaced words are called the **antecedent** of the pronoun. The antecedent of a pronoun is usually a noun and its modifiers, if any, but sometimes the antecedent can be a whole sentence.

> The dog lost *its* bone.
> (*Its* replaces *the dog.*)

> The old man, *who* had his car stolen, was in shock.
> (*Who* replaces *the old man.*)

> I have written to my younger sister, who lives in Las Piedras, to invite *her* to the wedding.
> (*Her* replaces *my younger sister, who lives in Las Piedras.*)

Do you want a small cone or a large *one*?
(*One* replaces *cone*. It is a special pronoun that allows the user to replace the noun and retain its modifiers.)

Lumsden tried to calm his wife's fears. He found *this* harder than he expected.
(*This* replaces the whole sentence dealing with an attempt to calm fears.)

Personal Pronouns

The personal pronouns are distinguished by person, case, and number.

FIRST PERSON
(the person speaking or writing)

Case	Singular	Plural
Nominative	I	we
Possessive	my, mine	our, ours
Objective	me	us

SECOND PERSON
(the person addressed)

Case	Singular	Plural
Nominative	you	you
Possessive	your, yours	your, yours
Objective	you	you

In the third person, pronouns are also distinguished by gender.

THIRD PERSON
(the person, place, or thing spoken or written about)

Case	Singular			Plural
	MASCULINE	FEMININE	NEUTER	
Nominative	he	she	it	they
Possessive	his	her, hers	its	their, theirs
Objective	him	her	it	them

Relative Pronouns

When a sentence is embedded inside another sentence to function as a relative clause, a relative pronoun replaces the repeated noun in order to make the new sentence grammatical.

> *Michael Jordan—Michael Jordan has all the moves—could not be stopped.

> Michael Jordan, *who* has all the moves, could not be stopped.

> *The tools—he bought the tools yesterday—were specked with rust.

> The tools *that* he bought yesterday were specked with rust.

Who, whom, whose, and *that* refer to people; *which* and *that* refer to things. Sometimes the relative pronoun can be omitted altogether: *The tools he bought yesterday were specked with rust.*

Interrogative Pronouns

The interrogative pronouns *who, whom, whose, what,* and *which* are some of the words that introduce questions. *Who, whom,* and *whose* indicate that the expected answer will be a person; *what* indicates that the answer will be something nonhuman; *which* may be used for either persons or things.

> *Who* was the chairman?   Answer: John

> *What* was he carrying?   Answer: a suitcase

> *Which* of the girls was hurt?   Answer: Justine

Demonstrative Pronouns

The demonstrative pronouns *this, these, that,* and *those* indicate nearness to or distance from the speaker, literally or figuratively. The antecedent of the pronoun usually is in another clause or sentence. Sometimes the reference is too general for there to be a specific antecedent.

> *This* is my father, Mr. Rodriguez, and *those* are my children, Juanita and Armando.
> (The antecedent *Mr. Rodriguez* is literally nearer to the speaker than are his children.)

> Marcellus would climb trees at night. *This* disturbed his mother.
> (The antecedent of *this* is the sentence about Marcellus' nocturnal tree-climbing.)

> Be gentle to *those* who stay angry.
> (*Those* has no antecedent, in the normal sense of the word. The reference is limited by the following relative clause.)

When these pronouns modify nouns they function as adjectives: *this event, these children.* This function is discussed in the section on determiners.

Indefinite Pronouns

The indefinite pronouns are so named because their antecedents are usually vague or unknown. These are such words as *each, all, either, anyone, somebody, everyone, many, several.* Some indefinite pronouns form the possessive case in the same manner as nouns: *anyone's, somebody else's.*

Intensive and Reflexive Pronouns

Personal pronouns ending with *self* or *selves* (*myself, ourselves, itself,* and so on) have two functions. The first is to repeat the noun antecedent in order to emphasize and intensify the meaning: *Mary herself was responsible.* The second function is to turn the action back on the subject antecedent.

> *I* hurt *myself.*
> (*Myself* repeats *I,* but it functions as the object while the antecedent *I* functions as the subject.)

Myself should not be used in place of *me:* *He is going to the hockey game with Michelle and *myself.* [*Me* should be used.]

Pronoun Case

Case is a form change that denotes the relation of a noun or a pronoun to other words in the sentence. In English, nouns have only one form change that could be called a case change—the apostrophe form (possessive case). The personal pronouns and the two relative pronouns *who* and *whoever* change form to indicate whether the case is subjective, objective, or possessive.

The Nominative or Subjective Case

The pronoun forms *I, we, you, it, he, she, they, who,* and *whoever* are in the nominative case. The uses of the nominative case follow:

➤ *Expressing a subject:*

> Jason and *I* are going to the pizza parlor.
> (*Me and Jason and *Jason and me are not acceptable in the standard English.)

I don't know *who* stole the peach tree.
(*Who* is the subject of *stole.*)

Give it to *whoever* comes.
(*Whoeve*r is the subject of *comes,* not the object of *to.*
The object of *to* is the whole clause *whoever comes*.)

➤ *Expressing the subject repeated:*

Three members of our club gave woodwind
recitals—Glynis, Paul, and *I.*
(The subject is repeated by *Glynis, Paul, and I.* This
repeated structure is called an **appositive.**)

➤ *Expressing the subject when the verb is omitted:*

He is more articulate than *she.*
(The verb *is* has been omitted.)

He plays as well as *I.*
(The verb *play* has been omitted. Many speakers find
this construction unduly self-conscious, so they add a
word that takes the place of the repetitive verb: He *plays
as well as I do*.)

➤ *Coming after the verb **be**:* Some educated speakers find
the nominative case after *be* so artificial that they will
sometimes prefer to use the objective form of the pronoun even though they are not following the rules of
standard English.

It was *they* who found the dog.

That must be *she.*
(OBJECTIVE: That must be *her.*)

It is *I.*
(OBJECTIVE: It is *me.*)

I shouldn't care to be *he.*
(OBJECTIVE: I shouldn't care to be *him.*)

The Objective or Accusative Case

The pronoun forms *me, us, her, him, them, whom,* and *whomever* are in the accusative case. The pronouns *you* and *it* have the same form in the nominative and accusative cases. The same is true, in English, for all nouns. The uses of the accusative case follow:

➤ *Expressing the object of a verb, verbal, or preposition:*

> Shoving *me* before *him,* he forced *me* down the alley.

> My brother came between Carlos and *me.*
> (Sometimes people will say **between Carlos and I* under the mistaken impression that polite people always say *I* rather than *me.*)

> *Whom* were they talking about?
> (*Whom* is the object of the preposition *about.* In writing, *whom* must always be used in this context. In speaking, *who* is becoming acceptable: *Who were they talking about?*)

> Give it to *whomever* he sends to your office.
> (*Whomever* is the object of the verb *sends.* Again, in speaking, *whoever* is becoming acceptable in this context.)

➤ *Expressing the object repeated:*

> The police ticketed three members of our group, Garcia, McEwan, and *me.*

> A lot of *us* kids were hurt in the accident.

➤ *Expressing the object when the verb is omitted:*

> Mr. Anderson did not recommend him as highly as *me.*
> (*As he did me* is also possible here.)

➤ _Expressing the nominal before the infinitive:_

> We wanted _him_ to suffer.
> (A nominal is a word that is not a noun but functions as one.)
>
> The plan was for _him_ to slide down the rope.

The Genitive or Possessive Case

There are two sets of pronoun forms in the genitive case:

1. my   our   your   her   his   its   their   whose

2. mine   ours   yours   hers   his   its   theirs   whose

The first set of pronouns function as noun modifiers (_his escape, my wife_) and are called here **possessives.** The second set of pronouns function as nominals. (This is _mine; Whose_ were found?) and are called here **independent possessives.**

   As we have seen, nouns and indefinite pronouns also have a genitive case. For convenience, examples of both nouns and pronouns will be given in this section on pronouns.

Functions of Possessives

➤ _Possessives function as determiners before nouns._ The meanings usually conveyed by these possessive determiners are possession, connection, the performer of an act, and the classification of a thing.

> _Whose_ car was stolen?
> (The question asks about the possession of a car.)

the *bureau's* lawyers

(The bureau does not possess the lawyers so much as the lawyers are connected to the bureau.)

➤ *Possessives function in gerund phrases as the introducer of the phrase.* They also function as the substitute for the nominative case that expresses the performer of the action. Thus *He was leaving* becomes *his leaving*.

His leaving at dawn upset his father.

He slipped away without *anybody's* noticing him.

The *girl's* singing of Brahms's "Lullaby" was beautiful.

(This gerund phrase must not be confused with a participle phrase, which in the following sentence modifies the nominative case *girl: The girl singing in the next room is my sister*.)

There are some exceptions to the rule that gerund phrases are started by a possessive noun or pronoun.

He slipped away without *anybody* in the room noticing him.

(The possessive form is not used because the pronoun does not immediately precede the gerund.)

Luis saw *him* leaving the parking lot.

(After verbs like *see, hear,* and *watch,* the objective form of the pronoun or noun is used.)

Throwing the bola is not easy.

(The action is so general that the writer has nobody in particular in mind. Therefore, no noun or pronoun introduces the gerund phrase.)

Functions of Independent Possessives

Independent possessives are nominals; that is, they function as subjects, objects, or complements as nouns do.

> I wonder *whose* this is.
> (*Whose* is the complement of the verb *is*. Note that this *whose* differs from the *who's* in *Who's there?*)
>
> *His* was a fascinating personality.
> (*His* is the subject of the verb *was*.)
>
> He's a friend of *Mother's* and *mine*.
> (*Mother's* and *mine* are the objects of the preposition *of*.)

THE VERB

The verb is a word or a group of words that usually express action or a state of being. There are two kinds of verbs that must be distinguished:

1. **The finite verb** works with the subject of the sentence to give a sense of completeness, a sense of a statement having been made.

2. **The nonfinite verb** or **verbal** functions as a nominal (something like a noun) or a modifier. It never works with a subject. It does not give a sense of completeness. Compare:

FINITE	NONFINITE
The documents *had incriminated* him.	the *incriminating* documents . . .
The authorities *accused* him of fraud.	the authorities, *having accused* him of fraud, . . .

The forms and functions of the finite verb are discussed in this section. Nonfinite verbs or verbals are discussed in Section 5.

Recognition of Finite Verbs

Finite verbs can be recognized by their form and their position in the sentence. Here are some of the things to look for when you are trying to identify the finite verbs in a sentence:

➤ Most finite verbs can take an *ed* or a *d* at the end of the word to indicate time in the past: *cough, coughed; celebrate, celebrated.* A hundred or so finite verbs do not have these regular endings.

➤ Nearly all finite verbs take an *s* at the end of the word to indicate the present when the subject of the verb is third person singular: *cough, he coughs; celebrate, she celebrates.* The exceptions are auxiliary verbs like *can* and *must.* Remember that nouns can also end in *s.* Thus *the dog races* can refer to a spectator sport or to a fast-moving third person singular dog.

➤ Finite verbs are often groups of words that include such auxiliary verbs as *can, must, have,* and *be: can be suffering, will have gone, must eat.*

➤ Finite verbs usually follow their subjects: *He* **coughs.** *The documents* **had incriminated** *him. They* **will have gone.**

➤ Finite verbs surround their subjects when some forms of a question are asked: **Is** *he* **coughing? Did** *they* **celebrate?**

Forms of the Finite Verb

Verbs are distinguished by number (singular and plural) and by person (first, second, third). In general, verbs have a different form only in the third person singular of the present tense.

> I, you, we, they *move.*
>
> BUT He, she, it *moves.*

An exception is the verb *to be,* which is more highly inflected:

> SINGULAR: I *am*; you *are*; he, she, it *is.*
>
> PLURAL: We, you, they *are.*

In a handbook such as this, it is impossible to present all of the possible forms of the verb. Instead, we will present the basic ingredients that make up the finite verb and give examples of the more common forms.

The finite verb can be a one-word verb with an indication of present or past tense: *watch, watched; freeze, froze.*

The finite verb can also be a group of words composed of one or more of the following ingredients:

1. **Modal auxiliaries:** *will, would, can, must,* etc.

2. **Perfect auxiliary:** a part of the verb **have** plus an **-en** or an **-ed** ending.

3. **Progressive auxiliary:** a part of the verb **be** plus an **-ing** ending.

4. **Passive auxiliary:** a part of the verb **be** plus an **-en** or an **-ed** ending.

5. **Main verb:** *watch, tolerate.*

The modal auxiliary is added to the main verb: (*may watch, must watch*). The perfect, progressive, or passive auxiliaries surround the next form of the finite verb. Some examples of this surrounding process follow:

> PERFECT: *a part of* **have** plus **ed** surrounding *watch*
> He **has** watch**ed** you.

> PROGRESSIVE: a part of **be** plus **ing** surrounding *watch*
> I **was** watch**ing** you.

> PERFECT: a part of **have** plus **en** surrounding *be;*
> PROGRESSIVE: a part of **be** plus **ing** surrounding *watch*
> I **had been** watch**ing** you.

Below is a layout of some forms of the finite verb *watch.* If all the modal auxiliaries, the singular and plural forms, and the past and present forms were presented, it would take pages to do so. Instead, the following list is limited to forms of the verb using the modal auxiliary *could* and some past forms not using *could.*

MODAL		PERFECT	PROGRESSIVE	PASSIVE
	had	watched		
	was		watching	
	was			watched
	had	been	watching	
	had	been		watched
could	watch			
could	have	watched		
could	be		watching	
could	be			watched
could	have	been	watching	
could	have	been		watched

Progressive perfect passive forms like *could have been being watched* are seldom used; therefore, they have been omitted from the paradigm.

Mood

A verb may be placed in the indicative, imperative, or subjunctive mood to indicate differences in the intention of the speaker or writer.

The indicative mood is used to make an assertion or ask a question.

The horse *galloped* down the street.

Where *are* you *going?*

The imperative mood is used for commands, directions, or requests.

COMMAND: *Go* to the store and *order* a typewriter.

DIRECTION: *Turn* right at the next traffic light.

REQUEST: Please *answer* my letter.

Subjunctive Forms

The present and past tense forms of a verb are sometimes used to express matters that are not present or past in the usual sense. They are matters of urgency, formality, possibility, and unreality. The present and past tense forms of the verb used for the subjunctive are not the expected forms. These unexpected forms are called forms of the **subjunctive mood**. (The expected forms are called forms of the **indicative mood**.)

I demand that he *see* me immediately.
(The expected form would be *he sees. He see* conveys an urgent request, a command.)

I move that the motion *be* tabled.
(*Be tabled* rather than the expected *is tabled* expresses the formality desired.)

It was important that she *love* me.
(The present tense form expresses an urgency in the past. The expected past form that *she loved me* is factual rather than urgent.)

If she *were* to go, there might be trouble.
(*If she were* expresses a possibility in the future. There is no trace of past time in this unexpected past tense form.)

If he *were* talented, he could make money.
(The past tense form here indicates that at present he is not talented. It expresses an unreality, a contrary-to-fact situation.)

There are ways to express subjunctive meanings other than using past and present forms of the verb. Auxiliaries such as *might* and *should* can also be used: If you *had been presentable, I might have taken you to the party.*

Transitive and Intransitive Verbs

Verbs are classified as transitive or intransitive.

A transitive verb (*transit* means to *carry,* as in *rapid transit*) requires an object to complete its meaning. The object of a transitive verb is affected, however slightly, by whatever the verb expresses:

The hammer *struck* the anvil.
(The object, *anvil,* has been hit.)

Angela *read* the newspaper.
(The object, *newspaper,* has been read.)

John *has* a horse.
(The object, *horse,* is owned.)

An intransitive verb makes an assertion without requiring any object.

The clock *strikes.*

He *walks* down the street every evening.

The bird *is* on the fence.

A linking verb, a special kind of intransitive verb, is one which connects the subject to a noun, pronoun, or adjective in the predicate.

Sean *is* the president.
(*Is* connects *Sean* to *president. Sean* and *president* are the same person. A noun like *president* used after a linking verb is called a predicate nominative.)

In the next two examples, *bluejay* and *I* are predicate nominatives.

The bird *is* a bluejay.

It *is* I.

The most frequently used linking verb is *to be.* Other commonly used linking verbs are *become, seem, smell, look, grow, feel, sound, get, taste, appear.*

Many verbs are both transitive and intransitive. A good dictionary will indicate the differences in meaning. In *The hammer strikes the anvil,* the transitive verb *strike* means to *hit.* In a sentence such as *The clock strikes,* the intransitive verb *strike* means to *sound.* The transitive and intransitive meanings of the same verb may be similar, but they are never identical. The statement *He breathes* means that "he" is alive, but *He breathes the mountain air* refers to an experience that "he" is having.

The Passive Voice

Transitive verbs can be switched around from the **active voice** to the **passive voice** by a transformation that changes the form of the verb and moves the object into the subject's position. The old subject, if it stays in the sentence, becomes a prepositional phrase starting with *by.* Thus, *The Yankees won the 1996 World Series* is transformed into *The 1996 World Series was won by the Yankees.*

The passive voice is used to emphasize or direct attention to the receiver of the action, in this case *the 1966 World Series.* The passive transform switches our attention from *The Yankees* to what they won: *the 1996 World Series.*

The passive voice is also used to eliminate the necessity of naming the agent of the action when that agent is unknown or unimportant.

The jury declared O. J. Simpson not guilty in 1995.

O. J. Simpson *was declared* not guilty in 1995.

Someone stole our car yesterday.

Our car *was stolen* yesterday.

Present and Past Tenses

All main verbs are in either the present tense or the past tense: *watch, watched.* The word *tense* is also used for other forms such as perfect and progressive forms.

➤ *The present tense expresses any time which has some element of the present in it, no matter how small.*

This apple *tastes* good.   (a present situation)

Apples *taste* good.   (a general truth)

Shakespeare *writes* in blank verse.
(He did so in the past, but this fact is still very relevant today.)

In *Hamlet,* the opening scene *takes* place at night.
(A play written in the past has a plot summary alive in the present.)

Rita *goes* to Mexico City tomorrow.
(The action will occur in the future, but there is a suggestion that the decision to go may have occurred in the present.)

He *uses* lemon in his tea.
(a habitual action, past, present, and future)

➤ *The past tense excludes the present and covers those events that took place at a definite time or habitually in the past.* As with the present tense, the meaning is sometimes reinforced by other words which indicate time.

I *went* down the street yesterday.
(a completed event in the past)

Whenever Rocky *went* down the street, the people cheered.
(a habitual action in the past)

Modal Auxiliaries

Modal auxiliaries express a wide variety of ideas and feelings. A few of the more common uses are listed here.

PERMISSION You *can* put your shirt on now.
You *may* come in.

ABILITY	I *can* read braille.
	She *could* open the door.
NECESSITY	He *must* see her today.
	He *had* to go to Nairobi.
CONCLUSION	He *must* have seen her.
GENERAL TRUTH	Cats *will* sleep for hours.

Future Time

Unlike Latin, English has no future tense. Instead, English uses modal auxiliaries, present and past tense forms, and adverbials of time to express future time.

He *is going to* lose his mind.

He *is about to* lose his mind.

I *begin* work *tomorrow*.

It's time you *went* to bed.

Shall and *Will*

To indicate simple futurity, formal usage dictates that *shall* is correct for the first person and *will* and *won't* are correct for the second and third persons.

I (we) *shall* (*shall not*) go.

You *will* (*won't*) go.

He (she, it, they) *will* (*won't*) go.

In recent years, *will* and *won't* are commonly used for all persons even in relatively formal writing. But the *shall* form has persisted in idiomatic expressions, so that *Shall we dance?* and *Shall we go?* are certainly more commonplace than the awkward sounding *Will we dance?* or *Will we go?*

To indicate a promise or determination, *will* is used in the first person: *I (we) will go.* To express a command or determination, *shall is* used in the second and third persons: *You (he, she, it, they) shall go.*

Perfect Tenses

A perfect tense is used to talk about an action that occurs at one time but is seen in relation to another time. *I ran out of gas* is a simple statement about a past event. *I've run out of gas* is a statement about a past event that is connected to the present.

I *have waited* for you.
(The present perfect indicates that the action occurred in the past and was completed in the present.)

Luis *has visited* San Juan several times.
(The action occurred frequently in the past so that it has become part of Luis' present experience.)

I *had waited* for you.
(The past perfect shifts the action further into the past so that it is completed in relation to a later time.)

Mary *had been* out in the canoe all morning when she suddenly fell into the lake.
(The past perfect indicates that, in the past, one event occurred before the other.)

By sundown he *should have finished* the job.
(The conditional perfect suggests that something else occurred at a later time to affect the completion of the job.)

By sundown he *will have finished* the job.
(The future perfect indicates that the event will be completed by a definite time in the future.)

Progressive Tenses

Progressive tenses draw our attention to the continuity of an action rather than its completion. A verb which in its own meaning already expresses a continuity does not need a progressive form. (*I live in Boston* already says it. *I am living in Boston,* the progressive form, says it twice.) But compare *He worked in his cellar* with the progressive form which stresses the continuity of the action: *He was working in his cellar.* The progressive is often helped out by adverbials which express continuity.

> He *is always running* to his mother.

> He *must have been painting* the house *for days now.*

> I'*ve been washing* the dog.
> (The combination of perfect and progressive paints a vivid picture of a man deeply involved in a past process of some duration with immediate relevance to the wet present.)

THE ADJECTIVE AND THE ADVERB

Because the adjective and the adverb have so much in common, it is best to discuss them at the same time.

Adjectives and adverbs identify the distinctive feature of something: the fastness of the horse in *the fast horse,* the fastness of the driving in *He drove fast,* the dishonor of the conduct in *dishonorable conduct,* the dishonor of the behaving in *He behaved dishonorably.*

Recognition of Adjectives and Adverbs

Adjectives and adverbs can be distinguished from each other by their form and their position in the sentence. Here are some ways of distinguishing these words.

➤ If a word fits one or both of the following blank positions, it is an adjective and not an adverb:

> He was very .... It was very ....
>
> He was very *cowardly.* It was very *swampy.*
>
> *He was very bravely. [adverb]
> (The adjective *brave* is needed to modify the pronoun *He*.)

Some adjectives, of course, will not fit these blanks because they should not be used with the intensifier *very.* (**He was very unique* is incorrect. Since *unique* means one of a kind, there are no real degrees of being *unique.*) More important, however, is the fact that other noun modifiers do not go in these blanks; therefore, this is a useful way to distinguish adjectives from other noun modifiers.

> *Because she was a *city* dweller, she was very *city.*
> (*City* can be a noun modifier, but it is not an adjective.)

> *Because it was a *gardening* tool, it was very *gardening.*
> (*Gardening* can be a noun modifier, but it is not an adjective.)

> Because he was a *jolly, green* giant, he was *green* and *jolly.*
> (*Green* and *jolly* are adjectives.)

➤ Adjectives and adverbs can sometimes be distinguished by form. Some of the several forms are listed below, including the most important one, which is that most adverbs are adjectives plus *ly*. (In a few cases both the adjective and the adverb end in *ly: cowardly, hourly*.)

	ADJECTIVE	ADVERB
theory [*noun*]	theoretical	theoretically
differ [*verb*]	different	differently
honor [*noun*]	honorable	honorably
coward [*noun*]	cowardly	cowardly
hour [*noun*]	hourly	hourly
collect [*verb*]	collective	collectively
back [*noun*]	backward	backward
shore [*noun*]		ashore
crab [*noun*]	crablike	crabwise

Although adverbs ending with *wise* have become popular, the reader may not be prepared for a particular noun's becoming an adverb. The following usage should be avoided: *The Giants did a remarkable job, special-teamwise.* Better: *The Giants' special teams did a remarkable job.*

The Article

The most used adjectivals are the articles, *a, an,* and *the. A* and *an* are called indefinite articles because they single out any one unspecified member of a class. *The* is called a definite article because it specifies a particular member or a particular group of members of a class.

A is used when it immediately precedes a word beginning with a consonant sound: *a book, a tree. An* is used when it immediately precedes a word beginning with a vowel sound: *an apple, an ancient city.*

NOTE: It is the sound, not the actual letter, that determines the form of the indefinite article: *a university, an NBA official, an 8-sided object.* In some instances when there are different pronunciations of the same word, the pronunciation used by the speaker or writer determines the form of the article. If the writer pronounces the word *humble* omitting the aspirant or *h*-sound, then the form *an humble person* may be used.

Functions of Adjectives

While adjectives and adverbs can perform the same functions (verb complements and modifiers), their functions are usually quite distinct.

Adjectives modify a noun or function as the complements of copulative verbs such as **be, seem, feel.**

The *old* man, *tired* and *surly,* waited for the return of his children.
(*Old, tired,* and *surly* modify the noun *man.*)

I am *happy* that he feels *good.*
(*Happy* and *good* are the complements of the verbs *be* and *feel.*)

Functions of Adverbs

Adverbs modify verbs and other modifiers.

He spoke to her *quietly.*   (modifies the verb *spoke*)

She sang *extremely* well.   (modifies the adverb *well*)

Comparison of Adjectives and Adverbs

Adjectives and adverbs have positive, comparative, and superlative forms. The positive form is the basic word: *small, beautiful, lush, loudly.*

For adjectives of one syllable, the comparative is usually formed by adding *-er* to the positive form: *small, smaller; lush, lusher.* The superlative form of one-syllable adjectives is usually made by adding *-est* to the positive form: *small, smaller, smallest; lush, lusher, lushest.*

For most adjectives of more than one syllable and for most adverbs, the comparative and superlative are formed by combining *more* and *most* with the positive form: *beautiful, more beautiful, most beautiful; loudly, more loudly, most loudly.*

Some adjectives and adverbs do not follow these rules.

POSITIVE	COMPARATIVE	SUPERLATIVE
happy	*happier*	*happiest*
little	*littler*	*littlest*
bad	*worse*	*worst*
ill	*worse*	*worst*
good	*better*	*best*
well	*better*	*best*

Functions of Adjective and Adverb Comparison

The comparative form indicates a comparison of two things or two groupings of things. Usually the two things or groupings of things are mentioned explicitly in the sentence, but this is not always so.

She ran *faster* than her mother.

I've tasted *sweeter* raspberries than these.

After that restful night, he was *more relaxed* when we came to see him.

(The comparison of two emotional states is implicit. The previous emotional state is implied, not stated.)

The superlative form is used when more than two things are compared.

She was the *fastest* reader in her family.

The *outermost* island was concealed by the approaching storm.
(Some other superlatives that end with *most* are *uppermost, innermost, westernmost,* and *foremost*)

She shouted *the most loudly* of them all.
(Some writers prefer to express the adverbial by means of an adjective form: *She shouted the loudest of them all.*)

Confusion of Adjectives and Adverbs

Some words like *fast, slow, very,* and *late* function as either adjectives or adverbs.

ADJECTIVE: It was a *fast* train. (modifies noun *train*)

ADJECTIVE: The clock was *fast.*
(complements verb *was*)

ADVERB: The horse ran *fast.* (modifies verb *ran*)

The following adjectives and adverbs are sometimes confused: *good, well, bad, badly. Good* is an adjective and functions as an adjective.

He was a *good* man. (modifies noun *man*)

I feel *good.* (complements verb *feel*)

Well is an adjective meaning in good health and may be substituted for *good* in the preceding examples. But *well* is also an adverb meaning in a satisfactory or superior manner.

He played *well.* (modifies verb *played*)

He was *well* aware of his plight.
(modifies adjective *aware*)

The adverb *badly* is sometimes mistaken for the adjective *bad*, meaning in poor spirits, in such sentences as *John feels bad, You look bad.* In both of these sentences, the adjective *bad* describes the condition of the subject (*John, you*). Never write: **I feel badly.* However, *He was badly mistaken* is correct.

When an adjective follows a linking verb (like *is, feel, look, seem, become, smell*), it complements the verb and is known as a predicate adjective.

The water is (seems, feels, looks, is getting, is becoming) *hot.*

I feel (look, am) *fine, ill, sick, good, bad.*

You look *beautiful.* (not *beautifully*)

THE VERBAL

Verbals are verbs which have lost their subjects, their capacity to indicate definite time, and their capacity to express such ideas as necessity, obligation, and possibility.

The Infinitive

The infinitive is the most versatile of the three verbals. It can be both active and passive, perfect and progressive.

To live happily is not so hard.
(present active form indicating present time)

To be living today is not so bad.
(present progressive active form indicating a continuous action in the present)

He was pleased *to have been recommended.*
(perfect passive form indicating two different times in
the past)

To have been recommended would have pleased
him.
(perfect passive form indicating that a past action could
have happened, but didn't. This is a subjunctive use of
the infinitive.)

The *to* in the infinitive is sometimes omitted. Compare:
*Ask me to do it, Let me do it; He was made to confess,
They made him confess.*

The Present Participle

The name of this participle is misleading. It can indicate
not only the present but also the past and the future.

Arriving early, they smiled with embarrassment.
(The actions are both in the past.)

Arriving tomorrow, they will be met at the airport.
(The actions are both in the future.)

The present participle has a perfect form in which the
auxiliary **have** plus the **-en** or **-ed** form of the verb is
used.

Having arrived early, they decided to wait for their
host.
(The actions are at different times in the past.)

The Gerund

The gerund is a present participle that functions as a
noun and therefore names an action or a state of being.
Like the infinitive, it may have modifiers and
complements.

Swimming is good exercise.

Eating too much is bad for one's health.

Being gloomy was habitual to her.

Shooting basketballs was his favorite pastime.

The Past Participle

The past participle can indicate past, present, and future meanings.

Thus *deceived,* he will be outraged.
(both actions in the future)

Baffled by your attitude, I cannot help you.
(both actions in the present)

Baffled by your attitude, I could not help you.
(both actions in the past)

The past participle has both perfect and progressive forms.

Having been discovered, the thief confessed.

Being watched, he could only pretend to be nonchalant.

Functions of Verbals

Because they have lost their subjects and their tense, verbals never function as do finite verbs. Instead, they function as nominals (structures that behave like nouns) or as modifiers. Usually they carry along with them their own modifiers and verb completions.

When the present participle works as a nominal, it is called a **gerund.** The infinitive working as a nominal is still called an infinitive. Some of the more common uses of the verbal follow:

➤ *Verbals as nominals:*

> *Being watched* made him nervous.
> (gerund as subject)
>
> *To be watched* made him nervous.
> (infinitive as subject)
>
> He was praised for his *typing*.
> (gerund as object of a preposition)
>
> He urgently desired *to confess*.
> (infinitive as object of a verb)

➤ *Verbals as modifiers of nouns:*

> His desire *to confess* was urgent.
> (modifies *desire*)
>
> The *incriminating* documents could not be found.
> (modifies *documents*)
>
> The statement *typed* earlier that morning had been mislaid.
> (modifies *statement*)

➤ *Verbals as modifiers of verbs:*

> He went to the mountains to *meditate*.
> (modifies *went*)
>
> He scored his thousandth point to *lead* the league.
> (modifies *scored*)

➤ *Verbals as modifiers of adjectives:*

> He was anxious *to cooperate*.
> (modifies *anxious*)
>
> The man, eager *to see* what was going on, looked inside.
> (modifies *eager*)

To lead the league, to see what was going on, and *typed earlier that morning* are verbal phrases, that is, verbals with their modifiers and their verb completions.

PREPOSITIONS AND CONJUNCTIONS

Prepositions and conjunctions are relationship words that are used to connect elements in the sentence. Relative pronouns have already been discussed in this context. Prepositions and the several kinds of conjunctions perform different functions and should be carefully distinguished from one another.

Recognition of Prepositions and Subordinating Conjunctions

Prepositions and subordinating conjunctions can be distinguished from each other by what follows them and by the fact that there are a limited number of subordinating conjunctions.

➤ *The preposition is followed by a nominal.* The nominal can be a noun, pronoun, gerund phrase, or noun clause.

> *because of* the bad weather
> (The noun *weather* is the object of the preposition *because of.*)

> *before* leaving home
> (The gerund phrase *leaving home* is the object of the preposition *before.*)

> *after* what he had done
> (The noun clause *what he had done* is the object of the preposition *after.*)

➤ *The subordinating conjunction is followed by a subject-verb structure with no other relationship word involved.*
Thus *he had done* can follow a subordinating conjunction, and *what he had done* can follow a preposition.

> *because* the weather was bad
> (*Because* is a subordinating conjunction introducing the subordinate clause.)

> *before* he left home
> (*Before* is a subordinating conjunction introducing the subordinate clause.)

Before, after, since, as, until are both preposition and subordinating conjunction depending on what follows: *Since this morning; since you went away.*

➤ *"If," "when," "while," "although" and some others are subordinating conjunctions that can have their subject-verb structures transformed so that they begin to look like prepositional phrases.*

> When you were mopping the floor
> When mopping the floor

> If it is at all possible
> If at all possible

> although he was very angry
> although very angry

Because these conjunctions cannot easily take nouns after them (**when dinner*), they are being called conjunctions here, but it would be no great disaster if *when mopping the floor* were to be called a prepositional phrase.

➤ *Most prepositions and subordinating conjunctions by their function are not easily confused with one another.*

The lists that follow are incomplete, but they do indicate the variety of structures that can be called prepositions and subordinating conjunctions.

PREPOSITIONS	SUBORDINATING CONJUNCTIONS
in	if
by	why
for	how
beneath	although
because of	because
in spite of	inasmuch as
considering	provided that
aboard	where
except	that
than	than
as	as

Despite the sustained campaign of advertising agencies, *like* is still a preposition in Standard American English.

> *Like* I was saying, it's going to rain.
> (*As I was saying* is the preferred form.)

> *Like* me, Hans enjoyed soccer.

> *Samsons smell good *like* a walnut should.
> (*As a walnut should* is still preferred in standard English.)

Coordinating Conjunctions

Coordinating conjunctions join sentence elements of equal importance. These conjunctions are *and, but, or, nor, for,* and *yet.* They may join a word to another word (*bread and butter*), a phrase to another phrase (*into the oven or over the fire*), an independent clause to another independent clause (*He wanted to learn, but he hated to study*), a dependent clause to another dependent clause (*Matilda came in after I arrived but before dinner was served*).

Coordinating conjunctions are occasionally used effectively to introduce a sentence.

> He said he would do it. *And* he did.

> She swore that she told the truth. *Yet* she lied.

Correlative Conjunctions

Correlative conjunctions are pairs of words used to join sentence elements of equal importance. They are words like *both . . . and, either . . . or, neither . . . nor, not only . . . but also.*

> *Either* you go now, *or* you stay here forever.

> *Not only* was the team weak offensively, *but also* they were inept defensively.

SENTENCE CONNECTORS

Sentence connectors join whole statements in clause or sentence form. Because some of these relationship words have adverbial forms (*obviously, naturally, unfortunately*), they are sometimes called **conjunctive adverbs.** The most common sentence connectors are *therefore, however, consequently, thus, then, in fact, moreover, nevertheless, so, in addition, meanwhile.* When they join independent clauses, they work with a semicolon. When they relate sentences, a period is used.

We watched his folly develop; *in fact,* we nurtured it.

Joe Louis was a fantastically successful boxer. *However,* he did not emerge from his great career a rich man.

Unlike coordinating conjunctions, some sentence connectors can be inserted appropriately within the structure of the second statement.

She was not pleased by his skating technique. She was delighted, *however,* by his self-control and poise.

THE INTERJECTION

Interjections (the word means *thrown in*) are words which do not fulfill any of the functions of the previous parts of speech. They are such words as *yes, no, oh, ah, well, hello.* Although they are frequently used in sentences, they are not properly parts of the sentence structure and are, therefore, separated from the remainder of the sentences by punctuation marks.

Oh, I didn't see you.

Yes, I'll do it.

I waited, *alas,* too long.

No! you can't mean it.

Chapter 2

The Sentence and Its Parts

When we are speaking, our sentences can be quite short. One side of a telephone conversation will reveal things like "Yes . . . sure . . . why not . . . OK, about five o'clock." However, usually, when we speak and always when we write, our sentences are longer, having a subject and a predicate.

THE SUBJECT AND THE PREDICATE

The sentence has two parts. The topic of the sentence is the **subject.** What is said about the subject is the **predicate.** Usually, but not always, the subject identifies the agent of the action; that is, it tells us who or what is doing something.

SUBJECT	PREDICATE
The delegates	arrived this morning.
San Juan	is the capital of Puerto Rico.
Grambling, a small black college in Louisiana,	has produced many outstanding professional football players.
The city	was designed to include many beautiful parks.

[The subject of the sentence is *the city,* but the city didn't do anything. Something was done to the city by persons unspecified.]

The Positions of the Subject and the Predicate in the Sentence

Nearly always the subject of the sentence comes first. There are occasions, however, when the subject does not come first.

➤ Occasionally for purposes of emphasis, the natural word order will be changed so that the predicate comes first.

> *Fred McGriff roared into third base*.
> (no emphasis)

> Into third base roared Fred McGriff.
> (emphasis on the predicate, which comes first)

➤ In sentences that ask questions rather than make statements, the subject can come first, but the more usual order is to place the subject inside the verb.

> *Your mother* is coming today?

> Is *your mother* coming today?

➤ In sentences that give commands rather than make statements, again the subject can come first, but, nearly always, the subject and part of the verb are deleted.

> *You* will do as I tell you!

> Do as I tell you!

➤ Sometimes, the subject can be moved out of its initial position, and a word that is lexically empty (that is, it has no meaning at all) takes its place.

> *To see you* is nice.
> (*To see you* is the subject of the sentence.)

It is nice *to see you.*
(*To see you* is still the subject of this sentence.)

Twelve players were on the field.
(*Twelve players* is the subject of the sentence.)

There were *twelve players* on the field.
(*Twelve players* is still the subject of the sentence. More-over, because it is a plural subject, it makes the verb plural. Compare: There *was* one player on the field.)

Forms of the Subject

The subject of the sentence has several forms. The most frequent forms are nouns, proper nouns, and pronouns.

We shall overcome.
(personal pronoun functioning as the subject)

Who is on third base?
(interrogative pronoun functioning as the subject)

Marcus Garvey was a charismatic leader.
(proper noun functioning as the subject of the sentence)

Those comments annoyed Jack.
(noun functioning as the subject of the sentence)

Occasionally, larger structures, such as noun clauses, gerund phrases, and infinitive phrases, can function as the subject of a sentence. For convenience, nouns, pronouns, and these larger structures are called **nominals.**

What she did annoyed Jack.
(noun clause functioning as the subject)

Playing chess amused Jack.
(gerund phrase functioning as the subject)

To collect every stamp issued by Mexico was Juan's ambition.

(infinitive phrase functioning as the subject)

Simple and Complex Subjects

The noun or pronoun by itself is the **simple subject.** This subject is important to identify because it controls the form of the verb. The simple subject and the verb form it controls are in boldface type in these examples:

One of *the ships* **is** sinking.

The **mayor,** *as well as the councilmen,* **has** been implicated.

The noun phrase—that is, the noun and all its modifiers—is the **complete subject.** The complete subject (except for the boldface simple subject) is italicized in the examples above and below.

The **furniture**, *which they had bought on Monday,* was delivered on Friday.

The Compound Subject

Sometimes more than one nominal can be used as the subject of the sentence. The combination of several nominals to express the topic of the sentence is called a **compound subject.**

The **drivers** *and the* **loaders** have threatened to strike.

Not only the **price** *but also the* **quality** *of their products* fluctuates wildly.

What he did *and* **what he said** were not the same.

Forms of the Predicate

The predicate, what is being said about the topic of the sentence, always has a verb. The verb usually has a verb completion called an **object** or a **complement.** Like the noun or the pronoun, the verb often has modifiers. The predicate of the sentence is, in effect, made up of a verb, a verb completion, and some verb modifiers. The various forms of the predicate depend on the kind of verb involved and the kind of verb completion.

Predicate with a Transitive Verb

The most frequent form of the predicate is one where the verb expresses some kind of action and is followed by a nominal. This nominal is called the **object;** the verb is called a **transitive verb.**

In the following sentences the verbs *brought, tuned,* and *said* are transitive verbs. The nominals functioning as the objects of these verbs are italicized.

They brought *their guitars* with them.

Juanita tuned *the piano.*

After the party Jack said *that they would have to clean the place.*

NOTE: Most transitive verbs must be completed by their objects. The following examples are not complete English sentences. (To show this, they are marked with an asterisk.)

   *They brought with them.

   *Juanita tuned.

   *After the party, Jack said.

Some transitive verbs can drop their objects and still make sense. *They have been celebrating* is as grammatical as *They had been celebrating his birthday.*

Some transitive verbs use two verb completions: a **direct object** and another structure called an **indirect object** or a **complement**, to refer to the object and complete the meaning of the verb. Both structures are needed to complete the thought. Compare:

*He gave his teacher.	He gave his *teacher* the *book*.
	(indirect object and direct object)
*The problem made Jack.	The problem made Jack *sweat*.
	(infinitive phrase *(to) sweat* as the complement)

➤ Nouns, pronouns, and prepositional phrases starting with *to* or *for* can function as **indirect objects.**

Eliseo gave twenty pesos to *his brother*.

Eliseo gave *his brother* twenty pesos.

Luis cooked a meal *for his sister*.

Luis cooked *his sister* a meal.

He called *her* a taxi.

➤ Nouns, pronouns, prepositional phrases, adjectives, and verbal phrases can function as **complements.**

He called her a *star*.

(The complement a *star* refers to the object *her;* they identify the same person. This can easily be confused with the two-object form above: *He called her a taxi.*

[*You're a taxi* is not what is meant here!] A lot of bad television jokes are based on this confusion.)

He thought the whole thing *a bad joke.*
(The noun *joke* and its modifiers function as the complement.)

They made her *taste the papaya.*
(infinitive phrase *(to) taste the papaya* as the complement)

I made him *sick.*
(adjective as the complement)

They heard their father *leaving the house.*
(participle phrase as the complement)

He put the book *on the table.*
(The prepositional phrase *on the table* functions as the complement. Note how essential it is to the sentence: **He put the book.*)

Predicate with a Linking Verb

When the verb expresses being, seeming, or becoming, the verb is called a **linking verb.** These verbs are followed by a nominal, an adjective, or an adverbial. (An adverbial is anything that works like an adverb.)

Not many verbs function as linking verbs, but those that do are common and are used frequently: *be, seem, become, remain, appear, look, feel, sound, taste, smell, grow.*

Puerto Rico became *a commonwealth* in 1952.
(noun as complement)

Her point was *that Rocky Marciano was the greatest champion of all time.*
(noun clause as complement)

Juanita will be *at her music teacher's house.*
(The prepositional phrase is the complement. It is an adverbial telling where.)

The meat smelled *bad.*
(The adjective is the complement. People sometimes use the adverb *badly* here. This is wrong. The linking verb always takes an adjective rather than an adverb—even if it sounds bad!)

The careful use of adjectives after verbs marks one of the differences between standard and nonstandard usage. (Television commercials will sometimes use nonstandard forms, so do not trust them.) In standard usage, the adjective follows a linking verb; very seldom does it follow transitive or intransitive verbs. Compare these uses:

*He played *good.*	He played *well.*
*This razor shaves *painless.*	This razor shaves *painlessly.*
*She sings *beautiful.*	She sings *beautifully.*

Predicate with an Intransitive Verb

Some words do not need an object to complete them. These verbs can stand by themselves, or they are completed by an adverbial which indicates location or direction. The adverbial is called the **complement.** The verb, with or without the complement, is called an **intransitive verb.**

The situation deteriorated.
(Nothing completes the verb.)

The clouds vanished.
(Nothing completes the verb.)

He lay *down.*
(The adverbial *down* completes the verb. Note: One cannot say **He lay.* This verb needs a complement to indicate where he lay.)

He sat *on the desk.*
(The adverbial *on the desk* is the complement.)

Compound Predicate Verbs and Verb Completions
Sometimes more than one verb or verb completion can occur in the predicate of the sentence. These structures are called the **compound verb,** the **compound object,** or the **compound complement.**

Their French heritage made *Henri* and *Camille* proud.
(two nouns functioning as the compound object)

Jack *fell* down and *broke* his crown.
(two verbs functioning as the compound verb)

His stupid remark made her *angry* and *dangerous.*
(two adjectives functioning as the compound complement)

Phrases and Clauses

As we have seen already, words work together in groups that can be moved around as single units.

Someone had slashed *the furniture, which they had saved so hard for,* with a knife.

The furniture, which they had saved so hard for, had been slashed with a knife.

In the garden was a statue.

A statue was *in the garden.*

These moveable groups of words are called phrases and clauses. A brief listing of the word groups that are recognizable as particular kinds of phrases and clauses follows. Sometimes these word groups are recognizable because of their form, sometimes because of their function. All of these phrases and clauses have been mentioned in passing in previous sections.

Phrases

Phrases are groups of words that do not have a subject and finite verb. Within them, however, can be inserted other structures that do have subjects and verbs.

➤ *A prepositional phrase* is a preposition followed by a nominal as its object. This phrase has too many functions to be of help in recognizing it.

> Stop *at the count of ten.*
> (The prepositional phrase has another prepositional phrase inside it and functions as a modifier of the verb *stop*.)

> The speaker was a woman *of extraordinary eloquence.*
> (The prepositional phrase modifies the noun *woman*.)

> He gave money to *whoever asked for it.*
> (The prepositional phrase has a clause with a subject and verb inside it. The phrase functions as an indirect object.)

➤ *A participle phrase* starts with a present or past participle. It modifies a noun or pronoun which is implicitly involved in the action expressed by the participle.

> *Holding the dog by its collar,* the boy refused to let go.
> (The participle phrase modifies *the boy*, the person holding the dog.)

Pulled tight across the frame, the material looked more lustrous.
(The participle phrase modifies *the material,* the substance which had been pulled tight.)

He was a man *long admired for his patience.*
(The participle phrase modifies *a man,* the person who had been admired for a long time. Note that *long,* the modifier of the participle, comes before it.)

➤ *A gerund phrase is* a participle phrase which functions as a nominal.

Using profane language is not permitted here.
(The gerund phrase is the subject of the verb *is permitted.*)

He caused the confusion by *suddenly changing lanes.*
(The gerund phrase sits inside a prepositional phrase as the object of the preposition.)

➤ *An infinitive phrase* starts with an infinitive. Sometimes the **to** of the infinitive form is omitted.

It was our desire *to serve humanity.*
(The infinitive phrase functions as the subject of was.)

I have a bone *to pick with you.*
(The infinitive phrase modifies *bone.*)

He wanted *to see if the young birds had left the nest.*
(The infinitive phrase is the object of *wanted.* It has inside it a clause with a subject and verb.)

We watched the bird *feed its young.*
(The infinitive phrase is the objective complement of the verb *watched.*)

➤ A *noun phrase is* a noun with its determiner and its modifiers. It is the noun phrase, not the noun, which is usually replaced by a pronoun.

> *The furniture, which they had saved so hard for,* had been slashed with a knife. There was no doubt that *it* had been irretrievably ruined.
>
> (The noun phrase is the noun, its determinant *the,* and the relative clause modifying *furniture.*)

> *His best six young black-and-white grazing dairy cows in the lower field, which have not yet been milked,* are getting noisy.
>
> (This artificial example is presented here to show that a noun phrase can have a considerable number of noun modifiers in it.)

➤ A *verb phrase* is not easy to define, because grammarians cannot agree on what to recognize as a verb phrase. There are at least three different patterns currently in use. Here we describe the verb phrase as a main verb and its auxiliaries: She *could have been watching* him.

Clauses

Clauses are groups of words that have subjects and finite verbs. Usually clauses are introduced by such relationship words as *who, that, so that, where, but, and, however.* Clauses can stand by themselves, or they can be dependent on other structures.

Independent Clauses

An independent clause can stand by itself. In this case, it starts with a capital letter and ends with a period (.), a question mark (?), or an exclamation point (!). It is called a sentence.

> Hold tight!   She's pretty.   Who did it?

An independent clause can be joined to another independent clause by punctuation, coordinating conjunctions, or sentence connectors.

Mrs. Butler spends lavishly; she has an independent income; unfortunately, she has no taste.

An independent clause can work with dependent clauses and can have dependent clauses inserted within itself.

When she got there, *she discovered that the cupboard was bare.*
(The independent clause has inside it a dependent clause functioning as the object of the transitive verb.)

Dependent Clauses
Like phrases, dependent clauses function as nominals and as modifiers. A dependent clause can be sometimes recognized by its introductory relationship word. A clause starting with *because* is always an adverb clause. Equally often, however, a dependent clause has to be recognized by its function in the sentence. A clause starting with *that* can be a noun clause, an adjective clause, or an adverb clause. Only its use in a particular sentence can identify it.

➤ *Noun clauses* usually start with *that,* but they can start with relative pronouns like *who* or *what*, or they can start with subordinating conjunctions like it, *when, why, where,* or *how.* Noun clauses function as nominals.

They hoped *that the war would end soon.*
(object of the verb *hoped*)

How he escaped was stated in the report.
(subject of the verb *was stated*)

Knowing *who was cheating* disturbed him greatly.
(object of the participle *knowing*)

They made it clear *he should pay immediately.*
(objective complement of the verb *made.* Note that the
conjunction *that* has been deleted from the dependent
clause.)

➤ *Adjective clauses* nearly always start with relative pronouns, although these pronouns are sometimes deleted.
When the noun antecedent refers to a place or a time,
the adjective clause can begin with the subordinating
conjunctions *where* or *when.* Adjective clauses modify
nouns and pronouns and follow them as closely as
possible.

A man *I know* grows tomato plants *that never bear
fruit.*
(The adjective clauses modify *man* and *plants.* As these
clauses identify which man and which plants are being
talked about, they are called **restrictive clauses** and are
left unpunctuated.)

He spoke to the woman in the car *who was drinking
a can of soda.*
(modifies the noun *woman*)

My brother, *who is not very sentimental,* did visit the
Moravian village *where we were born.*
(The first adjective clause is set off by commas to indicate
that it is **nonrestrictive;** that is, it gives additional information rather than restricting the meaning of the noun.)

➤ *Adverb clauses* start with a variety of subordinating
conjunctions that usually indicate such meanings as
time, place, reason, manner, condition, and so on.
Adverb clauses function as modifiers of verbs, other
modifiers, and sentences.

He was bitter *that she had deserted him.*
(modifies the adjective *bitter*)

We should answer *when she calls.*
(modifies the verb *should answer*)

As she turned to go, she smiled at him.
(modifies the verb *smiled*)

As I have stated before, the cupboard was indeed bare.
(modifies the sentence itself)

Classification of Sentences by Clause Type

For easy reference, a sentence can be classified according to the distribution of independent and dependent clauses. A **simple sentence** is an independent clause (*Facts are stubborn things*). A **compound sentence** has two or more independent clauses (*There the wicked cease from troubling, and the weary be at rest*). A **complex sentence** has an independent clause and one or more dependent clauses (*When she got there, the cupboard was bare*). A **compound-complex sentence** has two or more independent clauses and one or more dependent clauses (*Jack fell down, and Jill came tumbling after because she was too busy watching Jack*).

Modification

As has been shown in previous sections, subjects, objects, complements, and finite verbs are the basic elements that work together to make up the sentence. **Modifiers,** on the other hand, depend on other structures for their existence in the sentence. In the first example below, the adjective *old* is the complement of the verb. In the second example, the meaning of *old* stays the same, but its function has changed. The adjective *old* now depends on, and is subordinate to, the noun *man.*

> The man is *old.*
> (adjective as complement)

> The *old* man is tired.
> (adjective as modifier of the noun *man*)

> The apartment *upstairs* was available.
> (adjective as modifier of the noun *apartment*)

> The apartment I wanted was *upstairs.*
> (adverb as complement)

> Someone was playing drums *upstairs.*
> (adverb as modifier of the verb *was playing*)

Modifiers of Verbs

Verb modifiers identify the distinctive features of the action or state of being expressed by the finite verb or the verbal. The modifiers tell where, when, why, how, how often, how much, with what results, and under what circumstances or conditions something occured.

The structures most frequently used as verb modifiers or **adverbials,** as they are sometimes called, are adverbs, nouns, prepositional phrases, infinitive phrases, and adverb clauses.

> *When he spoke,* they fell silent.
> (adverb clause of time modifying *fell*)

> They went to Carnegie Hall to *hear Luciano Pavarotti sing.*
> (infinitive phrase of cause modifying *went*)

Verb modifiers *frequently* occur *after the verb.*
(adverb of frequency and prepositional phrase of place
modifying *occur*)

Delighted *because she had arrived early,* he opened
the champagne.
(adverb clause of cause modifying the verbal *delighted*)

They arrived *this morning.*
(noun of time modifying *arrived*)

Position of Verb Modifiers

Most verb modifiers can move around the sentence
without changing their function or meaning: *He raised
his hand slowly. Slowly he raised his hand. He slowly
raised his hand.* A few verb modifiers do not move so
easily: *He arrived early. *Early he arrived. *He early
arrived.*

Modifiers of Nouns

Noun modifiers are divided into those that are noun
markers or **determiners** and those that identify
distinctive features in nouns and are called **adjectivals.**

Determiners

Determiners are noun modifiers that express large
general features such as definiteness, indefiniteness,
quantity, countableness, singularity, and plurality. The
most common determiners are articles (*the, a, an*),
demonstrative pronouns used as adjectives (*this, those*),
personal pronouns (*my, his*), and noun possessives
(*Ramon's, the child's*).

These determiners exclude each other. If one is used,
the other can't be: **the my chicken,*that his book, *the
this curfew.* (It is possible to say *this, the curfew,* but,
here, *this* is not a determiner.)

Other pronouns can function as determiners, and some of them can work together (*all my joys*). Some examples of single and multiple determiners follow below:

some examples
(an indefinite countable number of examples)

both the boys (two definite countable boys)

much courage (an uncountable amount of courage)

we Americans
(several definite Americans associated with the speaker)

you children
(several definite children)

five books
(a countable number of indefinite books)

five of the books
(a countable number of definite books)

Ramon's few enemies
(an indefinite number of countable enemies possessed by Ramon)

Some other words that work as determiners are: *other, many, another, any, several, more, most, first, last, second, third, enough, no, which, all, each, neither, either.*

Adjectivals
Adjectivals are noun modifiers that identify distinctive features in the nouns they modify. These distinctive features can range from such things as the ability to be parked in (as in *the parking lot*) to such things as physical condition, age, weather involvement, religious

posture, and identity (as in *the tired, old, rain-drenched, blasphemous man whom men called Lear*).

The structures most frequently used as adjectivals are adjectives, nouns, adverbs, prepositional phrases, participle phrases, infinitive phrases, and relative clauses.

Position of Adjectivals
Most adjectivals have a fixed position in the word order. They cannot move freely.

The pretty child	*the child pretty
The man, angry at his daughter	*the angry at his daughter man
the filled parking lot	*the parking filled lot

➤ *Short adjectivals, with the exception of adverbs, sit between the determiner and the noun.* Determiner and noun are given in boldface in the following examples.

the wounded marine **sergeant**

a tall, dark, distinguished **gentleman**

the beautiful red **dress**

the stimulating, intelligent **conversation** afterwards

the French language **teacher**

NOTE: There can be ambiguity when an adjective is followed by two nouns. In the preceding example, the teacher could be a Frenchman teaching German or someone of unspecified nationality who teaches the French language.

➤ *Most longer adjectives come after the noun they modify because they are derived from a sentence that is inserted after the noun.* This sentence or clause repeats the noun and usually uses the verb **be.**

> *Michael Jordan—Michael Jordan is one of the top basketball players—had a sensational game tonight.

To make the sentence grammatical, the inserted sentence is kept by replacing the repeated noun with a relative pronoun— to produce an adjectival relative clause.

> Michael Jordan, who is one of the top basketball players, had a sensational game tonight.

A second solution is to reduce the sentence to a phrase by deleting the repeated noun and the part of the verb **be.**

> Michael Jordan, one of the top basketball players, had a sensational game tonight.
> (The noun phrase following *Michael Jordan* is an adjectival modifying *Michael Jordan*. It is sometimes called an **appositive.**)

The following inserted sentences are transformed into various adjectivals that come after the noun they modify.

> *that car—that car is in the parking lot . . . that car *in the parking lot*   (prepositional phrase)

> *the car—the car was sold yesterday . . . the car *sold yesterday*   (past participle phrase)

> *the car—the car was to be sold tomorrow . . . the car *to be sold tomorrow*   (infinitive phrase)

> *our car—our car was purring gently . . . our car, *purring gently*   (present participle)

Participle phrases can move out of the position after the noun: *purring gently, our car* . . . In this situation the participle phrase can sometimes lose track of the noun it modifies and can "dangle."

Modifiers of Adjectives and Adverbs

Adjectives and adverbs are often modified by adverbs that indicate the comparative intensity of the quality involved. A man can be *slightly* tired, *somewhat* tired, or *very* tired. These adverbs are called **intensifiers.**

> She spoke *quite* firmly to him.
> (adverb somewhat intensified)

> He was *rather* quiet when she spoke.
> (adjective somewhat intensified)

> She was *extremely* happy to see him.
> (adjective very intensified)

> He was a *little* depressed.
> (adjective slightly intensified)

> As a result, they sang *much* more loudly.
> (adverb very intensified)

Quite a few words function as intensifiers, some polite and some indelicate. Every dialect has its favorite, sometimes faddish, intensifiers. Unless you are from Texas or Great Britain, do not write that you are *mighty* pleased or *frightfully* pleased to see your friends. In writing, *real* pleased and *sure* pleased are also dialect forms to be avoided.

Large Structure Modifiers of Adjectives and Adverbs

Certain adverbs like *so, more, such, as,* and a few adjectives like *glad, happy, disappointed, bitter, conscious, aware, similar,* and *different* can be modified by large structures such as the prepositional phrase and the adverb clause starting with the subordinating conjunctions *that, than,* and *as.*

➤ *When "so," "more," "such," and "as" modify an adjective, they usually require an adverb clause to indicate the nature of the comparison or the result involved.* The adverb clause is dependent on the adverb, not the adjective. Remove the adverb, and the adverb clause cannot stand after the adjective. **He was tired that he couldn't stand up.* [should be *so tired that*]

> He was *so* glad to see her *that he jumped over the sofa.*

> They had *such* bad weather *that they left after a week.*

> He was *as* angry *as he had ever been.*

> He was *more* upset *than she had expected.*

➤ *Some adjectives require a completion in a way that certain verbs do. It was ugly* is a complete statement; *it was similar* sounds incomplete. These "transitive" adjectives usually take a prepositional phrase or an adverb clause starting with *that.* These large structures are the modifiers of the adjective. (One or two grammarians are now calling them the "object" of the adjectives.)

> He was aware *of his weakness.*

> He was aware *that he had a weakness.*

> She was happy *about his buying the car.*

> She was happy *that he had bought the car.*

> She was happy *to see him.*

It was similar *to the others.*

He was different *from the other boys.*

Like some transitive verbs, some of these adjectives can stand by themselves without their modifiers. *He was devious, calculating, and bitter. After the catastrophe, she was happy.*

Chapter 3

Sentence Errors

A knowledge of words, phrases, clauses, basic structures, modification, and agreement is essential to good writing, but such a knowledge does not guarantee that our first drafts will not be confused and marred by writing errors. When we are thinking of several things at once and alternate wordings go racing through the mind, it is all too easy to write inaccurately. The painstaking correction of errors is an inevitable part of good writing. Only after this process of correction is completed by the writer can the reader concentrate on what we are saying rather than on how we are saying it.

In early drafting, whole sentences can go awry. To enable the reader to concentrate on the content of the material, the writing must contain complete, separate sentences. Fused sentences, comma faults, and sentence fragments are the sentence errors that most severely dislocate the continuity of the writing.

SENTENCE FRAGMENTS

Recognition of Sentence Fragments

When modifiers or nominals are too long, careless writers will sometimes allow them to break off from their sentences to stand by themselves. The modifier or nominal left standing alone is called a sentence fragment.

In the following example, an adverb clause is left standing by itself: *Because he was serving his residency at the overcrowded city hospital.* The reader is left in suspense, asking, "Well, what about it?" The writer may add a new sentence: *He had little leisure time,* but this is not a good repair job. The fragment still stands.

The Correction of Sentence Fragments

Sentence fragments can be corrected in two ways:

1. by properly relating the large modifier to its noun or verb or relating the large nominal to its verb.

2. by starting all over again and converting the modifier or nominal into a sentence which can stand by itself.

Below are examples of sentence fragments and illustrations of one or both methods of repair.

FRAGMENT adverb clause as modifier	*While millions of people all over the world are dying of starvation.
CORRECTION by first method	We have an abundance of food while millions of people all over the world are dying of starvation. (adverb clause modifier of *have*)
FRAGMENT infinitive phrase as modifier	*To hear Beethoven's piano sonatas played by a great pianist.
CORRECTION by first method	We went to Royce Hall yesterday evening to hear Beethoven's piano sonatas played by a great pianist. (infinitive phrase modifier of *went*)
FRAGMENT participle phrase as modifier	*Believing in equal opportunity for all.

CORRECTION by second method	My Congresswoman believed in equal opportunity for all. Therefore she was a strong advocate of a good civil rights bill. (verbal *believing* transformed into a finite verb *believed*)
FRAGMENT gerund phrase	*Giving an aggressive nation whatever it demands.
CORRECTION by first method	I do not advocate giving an aggressive nation whatever it demands. (gerund phrase object of *do not advocate*)
FRAGMENT noun phrase as modifier (appositive)	*A brilliant, hard-driving man who will not tolerate slackness.
CORRECTION by first method	The greatest influence on my life has been my Uncle Oscar, a brilliant, hard-driving man who will not tolerate slackness. (noun phrase modifier of *Uncle Oscar*)
CORRECTION by second method	Uncle Oscar is a brilliant, hard-driving man who will not tolerate slackness. He also happens to be the greatest influence on my life. (noun phrase transformed back to original sentence)

THE COMMA FAULT

When the writer uses a comma between two sentences, rather than relating them with a semicolon or a relationship word or separating them with a period,

space, and capital letter, the result is called a comma
fault or comma splice and can sometimes be confusing.

> *Classes will begin on September 19, the year
> 1997 should be a good one for all of us at Northern
> State.

Sometimes it is more obvious what the writer intends
to say.

> *We had taken the wrong turn, we found we were
> heading south instead of west.

The comma fault is easily repaired by making two
sentences out of the spliced sentences. *Classes will
begin on September 19. The year 1997 should be a
good one for all of us at Northern State*. If this solution
seems too abrupt, then one of the following methods of
coordinating two sentences should be employed.

> We had taken the wrong turn, *and* we found we
> were heading south instead of west.
> (coordinating conjunction *and* preceded by a comma)

> We had taken the wrong turn; we found we were
> heading south instead of west.
> (semicolon relating two sentences with similar content)

> We had taken the wrong turn; *thus* we found we
> were heading south instead of west.
> (sentence connector *thus* preceded by a semicolon)

THE FUSED SENTENCE

The fused sentence is two or more sentences run
together with no punctuation or spacing to separate
them. As a result, the reader, misled and confused,

must reread the sentence and, even then, may not always catch the writer's intent.

> *With gladness, we see the Christmas season approach Mrs. Dunkeld and I share our joy with you.

The quick cure for the fused sentence is to make two distinct sentences out of it.

> With gladness, we see the Christmas season approach. Mrs. Dunkeld and I share our joy with you.

If the two sentences sound awkward, then the use of relationship words such as coordinating conjunctions or sentence connectors may be in order.

> With gladness we see the Christmas season approach. Mrs. Dunkeld and I, therefore, share our joy with you.

Chapter 4
Logic and Clarity

The basic structures and modifiers of a sentence are bound together by meaning, relationship words, and word order. Another way of making the elements of a sentence cohere is the relating of significant forms. This relating of forms is called agreement.

AGREEMENT OF SUBJECT AND VERB

Agreement occurs when a structure changes its form because of the influence of another structure. In English, nominal subjects influence the forms of finite verbs; nominals also influence the forms of pronouns. In some European languages, a noun will influence the form of the article that comes before it. Thus in Spanish we find *la televisión* and *el fútbol: la* is used because the noun is feminine; *el* is used because the noun is masculine. In English, distinctions are occasionally based on gender, but number is the most common ground on which agreement is based.

Subject and Verb Agreement by Number

The rule for number agreement is not difficult. A singular subject requires a singular verb; a plural subject requires a plural verb. To apply the rule, however, you must be able to do three things: remember that the subject controls the verb form and not be distracted by other structures which may stand close to the verb; be able to determine the number of the subject; and finally, know the correct singular and plural forms of the verb.

Selection of the Subject to Control the Number of the Verb Form

In the sentence *One of our ships is missing* there is a temptation to let the plural noun *ships,* which stands by the verb, control the verb form because *ships is* sounds peculiar. The temptation must be resisted, for it is the more remote word *one,* the subject of the verb, which controls the number of the verb. There are several circumstances where another structure may distract the writer from remembering that the subject controls the number of the verb form.

➤ *The verb agrees with the subject, not with the elements in the modifier of the subject.*

> *Each* of the sofas *is* ninety inches long.
>
> A *swarm* of bees *is* coming towards us.
>
> The *men* in the district office *have* organized a ball team.
>
> (*Sofas, bees,* and *office* stand close to the verb, but they do not control the form of the verb; the subject does.)

➤ *The verb agrees with the subject even if the following modifier sounds and looks like a coordinator joining two nouns.* Several prepositions have a strong coordinating sense, such as *including, together with, along with, no less than, in addition to,* and *as well as,* but the verb that follows must agree with the noun subject that is modified by the prepositional phrase.

The *mayor,* as well as the councilmen, *has* been implicated.

(*Mayor* is the singular subject that controls the form of the singular verb *has been implicated.*)

➤ *The verb agrees with the subject, not with the following complement.*

The greatest *nuisance is* the refunds we have to make.

The *children* of today *are* the hope of tomorrow.
(The complement nouns *refunds* and *hope* do not control the verb form. To do so, they must be moved into the subject position of the sentence to become the subjects of their sentences: The *hope* of tomorrow *is* the children of today.)

➤ *If for any reason the subject is moved out of the subject position, it will still control the verb form as long as another nominal is not moved into its place.*

Ramon and Eduardo are at the jai alai game.

Where *are Ramon and Eduardo?*
(The sentence has been transformed into a question, and *Ramon and Eduardo* is still the subject of the sentence.)

There *were twelve players* on the field.
(*There* has been moved into the subject position, but it means nothing; it is an expletive, a space-filler, and *twelve players* is still the subject of the sentence as is *a fight* in the sentence *There was a fight on the field.* The subjects control the verb forms.)

There is one exception to the rule. The word *it* also can function as an expletive displacing the subject of the sentence. However, because it is also a singular pronoun, it controls the verb even if the subject is plural.

> *It is* ambitious executives who catch the early train.
> (*Ambitious executives* is the plural subject, but it is the expletive *it* that controls the verb form *is*.)

Usually the subject displaced by *it* is obviously singular so that it doesn't really matter what controls the singular verb form.

> It is rumored *that he is about to resign.*
> (The noun clause is the singular subject of the sentence.)

Selection of the Correct Number of the Noun Subject to Control the Verb Form

Most problems in subject-verb agreement occur because the number of the noun or nouns functioning as the subject is not always apparent. *The fish* can be singular or plural despite its singular form. *The news* is always singular despite its plural form.

➤ *Some nouns in the plural form can be singular in meaning, or they can be plural in meaning. Trousers, tongs, wages, tactics, pliers, scissors, odds* and *barracks* are plural in meaning. Therefore they require a plural verb.

> The scissors *are* in the lefthand drawer.

Billiards, news, mathematics, linguistics, mumps, and *measles* are singular in meaning. Therefore they require a singular verb.

> Measles *is* a communicable disease.
> (Some people do say, however, that *Measles are catching.*)

➤ *Some nouns in the plural form can be both singular and plural.* When they denote fields of knowledge or activity, they are singular; in most other uses, they are plural.

> Politics *has* always attracted persons of talent.

> The politics of the situation *are* complicated.

> Statistics *is* not always a dry subject.

> The statistics *were* largely erroneous.

➤ *Some nouns which specify an amount of something are singular when the things or people involved are regarded as a unit.* In this case, they take a singular verb.

> Two plus two *is* four.

> Two thirds of the sweater *has* been completed.

> Eight pounds of grapes *seems* a lot.

> Ten percent of their capital *has* been absorbed already.

> Ten percent of the men drafted *are* over thirty.
> (Here the men are regarded as individuals, not as a unit.)

➤ *Collective nouns are usually singular but can be plural.* If the collective is regarded as a unit, the collective noun is singular and requires a singular verb.

> The orchestra *performs* well under any conductor.

> The family *is* coming over this afternoon.

If, however, members of the collective are considered individually, the collective noun is plural and requires a plural verb.

The family *were* informed as soon as they could be reached by telephone.

(Members of the family were informed individually by means of several telephone calls.)

➤ *The number of some foreign plurals can be confused where a plural is mistaken for a singular.*

*The public media *is* in trouble.

(*Media* is plural in form and meaning; therefore the verb should be plural. *The public media are in trouble.*)

*This phenomena *fascinates* him.

(*These phenomena fascinate him.*)

Selection of the Correct Number of the Compound Subject to Control the Verb Form

➤ *A compound subject coordinated by "and" is nearly always plural and requires a plural verb form.*

Mink and sable *are* expensive furs.

The senator and his wife *were* warmly received.

If, however, the compound subject refers to just one person or thing, then the verb form is singular.

A scholar and a gentleman *is* what he strives to be.
(one person)

This prelude and fugue *is* by Bach.
(one composition)

When the compound subject refers to closely related things, it can be singular or plural depending on the closeness of the relationship. In borderline cases, the singular form of the following verb sounds better.

The courage and patriotism of De Gaulle *were* cherished by many Frenchmen in 1940.

(The two qualities are related but distinct from each other; so the plural verb form is used.)

The protection and feeding of young fledglings *is* the constant preoccupation of the adult birds.

(The two qualities seem so close that the singular verb form is used.)

➤ *Singular nouns coordinated by "or," "either . . . or," "neither . . . nor," or by "not only . . . but also" are regarded as a singular subject and require a singular verb form.*

Not only the mother but also the child *was* badly dehydrated.

Either the muffler or the tailpipe *was* replaced.

Neither time nor prosperity *has* softened his heart.

I think Armando or Helen *has* our passports.

When these coordinating conjunctions join plural nouns, the verb is plural. (*Neither the Saints nor the Packers are going to win this year.*) When these conjunctions join singular and plural nouns, then the verb agrees in number with the closer noun to it.

Neither his advisors nor the President himself *has* acted wisely in this crisis.

(*President* is closer to the verb.)

Either the cloth or the dyes *are* defective.

(*Dyes* is closer to the verb.)

Some writers dislike this construction and recast the sentence to avoid it.

Either the cloth *was* defective or the dyes *were*.

Selection of the Correct Number of the Pronoun Subject to Control the Verb Form

➤ *Most indefinite pronouns are regarded as singular pronouns and require a singular verb form.*

> *Somebody* across the street *is* playing a trombone.

> As yet *nobody* has challenged my theory.

> *Each* of the sofas *is* over ninety inches long.
> (The singular pronoun *each,* not the plural noun *sofas,* controls the verb form.)

> *Everybody* in the room *was* getting sleepy.
> (Despite the fact that *everybody* is obviously plural in meaning, it is a singular pronoun in standard English.)

Some of these indefinite pronouns can work as determiners before singular nouns, and although there may be a strong feeling that more than one thing is involved, the verb form is still singular.

> Neither idea *was* any good.
> (Although the speaker is talking about two ideas being no good, in standard English the verb form must be singular.)

> Each baby chick *was* inspected to establish its sex.
> (Thousands of chicks were probably being processed this way, but the singular noun *chick* and the singular meaning of *each* demand that the verb be singular in form.)

➤ *A few indefinite pronouns such as "many," "several," and "few" refer to more than one person or thing.* These pronouns are plural and take plural verb forms.

> Several *have* already been tested.

> Many *are* called, but few are chosen.

The nouns *variety* and *number* also take plural verb forms when they are preceded by *a*. When they are preceded by *the,* they are singular.

A variety of fish *abound* in these waters.

A number of horsemen *were* on the hill.

The number of horsemen on the hill *was* not great.

➤ *Like collective nouns, some indefinite pronouns can be either singular or plural depending on whether they refer to a quantity or individual units of something.*

Some of the cereal *is* stale.
(a quantity of cereal)

Some of the apples *are* rotten.
(several individual apples)

Most of the money *is* gone; so *are* most of the people.
(A quantity of money and several people have disappeared.)

The pronoun *none* behaves in a similar fashion; in addition, it can be singular when the meaning of *not one* of the individuals is intended.

Luckily, *none* of the property *was* damaged; *none* of the horses *were* hurt; but *none* of us *is* blameless in this matter.

➤ A *relative pronoun can be either singular or plural depending on the number of its antecedent. Sometimes the antecedent is not easy to find.*

She is one of those courageous *women who have* sacrificed their lives for equal rights.
(*Who* can refer in general for its meaning to *she, one,* or

women. Specifically it refers to the plural *women.*
Therefore the verb that the pronoun *who* controls is
plural.)

Selection of the Correct Form of the Verb to Agree with the Subject by Number

Singular and plural verb forms are usually not hard to
identify. The correct form means, in this context, the
form that is used in Standard American English. Many
dialects of English use other forms that are correct in
these dialects but are wrong if they are used in
Standard American English. Below are some verb
forms that are correct in their dialects but should not be
employed when using Standard American English.

*He *don't* know what he's doing.
(*Don't* is used as the third person singular form in many
English dialects. The correct form in Standard American
English is *doesn't. Doesn't* must always be used in the
standard dialect: *He doesn't know what he is doing.*)

*They *be* doing that all the time.
(*Be* is used as the third person plural form in some black
American dialects and in some British English dialects.
The correct form in the standard dialect is *are: They are
doing that all the time.*)

*I'm right, *amn't* I?
(*Amn't* is used as the first person singular form in some
Scottish dialects. *Ain't* is the accepted form in several
American and British dialects, but the correct standard
singular form is the plural form *aren't: I'm right, aren't I?*
This does not make a lot of sense, but one must remember
that language usage is not always logical.)

Subject-Verb Agreement by Person

In English, the person of the subject noun or pronoun has little effect on the form of the verb. Only one verb (**to be**) has several forms that change in accord with the first, second and third persons of pronouns: *I am, you are, she is, I was, you were.* Some auxiliary verbs are unchanged by the person of the subject: *I can, you can, she can.* All other verbs change only in relation to the third person singular of the present tense: *I talk, he talks.* This change is not observed in all dialects of English, but Standard American English demands a distinction between the two forms. **The man talk all night* is a serious error.

AGREEMENT OF PRONOUN AND ANTECEDENT

As was pointed out in Section 2, a pronoun is a word that sometimes lacks specific meaning. Most pronouns depend on another structure for their meaning. The other structure, the antecedent, controls the pronoun as regards number, person, and gender. Some of the pronouns that are controlled by their antecedents are the personal, demonstrative, and relative pronouns.

Selection of the Correct Pronoun Based on the Number of the Antecedent

➤ *Collective nouns can be singular or plural depending on whether the collective or the several individuals involved are emphasized.* The following pronoun will be singular or plural accordingly.

The staff expressed *its* confidence in *its* medical director.
(The staff acted collectively.)

The staff have been airing *their* grievances publicly.
(Individual staff members had been complaining.)

The committee submits *its* report annually.

He ordered the committee to cease *their* bickering.
(Many writers find this construction artificial and will insert the plural word *members* after *committee* to accommodate the plural pronoun *their*.)

NOTE: As regards gender, collective nouns are neuter, requiring the pronouns *it, its,* and *which*.

➤ *Indefinite pronouns are usually singular but can be plural depending on whether a quantity or individual units are emphasized.* The following pronoun will be singular or plural accordingly.

Some of the cereal has kept *its* freshness, but *some* of the apples have worms in *their* cores.
(The cereal is in quantity, the apples in individual units.)

Neither idea had any point to *it*.

Each of the sofas has lost *its* castors.

Everybody raised *his or her* voice in song.
(Occasionally the plural sense is so strong that some writers are tempted to use a plural pronoun. *Everybody grabbed their coats and ran.*)

NOTE: As regards gender, the masculine pronoun has traditionally been used to refer to an indefinite pronoun (like *everyone*); today, however, *his or her* is considered the preferred form to use when an indefinite pronoun is the antecedent: *Everyone is wearing his or her jogging suit to the picnic.*

➤ *A compound subject is singular when the coordinator is "or" and plural when the coordinator is "and."*

> The senator and his wife were warmly received after *their* world tour.

> Either Vincente or Martin may leave *his* children with us.

When one of the antecedents joined by *or* or *nor* is plural, the pronoun agrees in number with the closer antecedent.

> Neither the producer nor the *sponsors* admit *they* were aware of the fraudulent practices.

> Neither the sponsors nor the *producer* admits that *he* was aware of the fraudulent practices.

➤ *When the antecedent of the pronoun is a large structure like a sentence, the following pronoun is always singular.*

> Lumsden tried to calm the child's fears. He found *this* more difficult than he had expected.
> (Some writers are unhappy about a pronoun taking the place of a sentence and will insert a noun in order to avoid using a pronoun in this manner. *He found this activity more difficult than he had expected.*)

Selection of the Correct Pronoun Based on the Person and Gender of the Antecedent

As nearly all noun and pronoun antecedents are third person, there is seldom any problem in selecting the correct pronoun to follow them. *Mr. Riggs said that* **he** *would accept the chairmanship.* On rare occasions a second person pronoun will follow the name of a person. *Mr. Riggs,* **you** *come down here at once!*

As far as gender is concerned, English bases gender on sexual difference, whereas other European languages use arbitrary gender distinctions where football is masculine, television is feminine, and a girl can be neuter. In English, a masculine pronoun follows a male antecedent; a feminine pronoun follows a female antecedent; and a neuter pronoun follows nearly all other antecedents. Thus *a girl* is *she,* an uncle is *he,* and *a comb* is *it.*

Traditionally, masculine pronouns have been used to refer to abstract, singular nouns like *mayor, judge, professor, doctor, senator, employer, person,* and *reader:*

A judge must use *his* discretion in such a matter.

Since, today, women have assumed larger roles in many formerly masculine fields, the problem of sexist language arises. It can be solved in several ways:

➤ by using both third person singular pronouns:

A judge must use *his or her* discretion in such a matter.

➤ by using plural forms to avoid the singular human noun:

Judges must use *their* discretion in such matters.

➤ by the sparing use of *you:*

Once the writer has determined his purpose . . .

Once *you* have determined *your* purpose . . .

➤ by revising the sentence:

(a) The worker should divide his task . . .

The task should be divided . . .

(b) If the beginner is guided by these rules, he should be . . .

The beginner guided by these rules should be . . .

Selection of the Correct Pronoun Based on the Antecedent Being Human or Nonhuman

It and *its* are the pronouns used when the antecedent is nonhuman. However, animals whose sex is significant or who are well-known to the speaker can be called *he* or *she,* which are the pronouns used for antecedents that are human.

The relative pronouns *who, whom,* and *that* refer to antecedents that are human (or are familiar animals); *which* and *that* refer to antecedents that are nonhuman.

He is one of *those who* know all too well that the *memories which* move us fade all too fast.
(*Those* is the human antecedent of *who; memories* is the nonhuman antecedent of *which.*)

That can refer to both humans and nonhumans, and some good writers will use *that* interchangeably for *who* or *which.* However, it helps to use *that* when the clause it introduces establishes the identity of the antecedent and to use *who* or *which* when the antecedent already has its identity fairly well established.

A *man that* drinks and drives a *car that* has faulty brakes does not think much of *his wife, who* must sit at home listening to the sounds of night traffic. (*Man* and *car* need restrictive modifiers. The female human antecedent is already identified by the words *his* and *wife.*)

FAULTY PRONOUN REFERENCE

Pronouns lack specific meaning and must have antecedents to give them this meaning. Like dangling modifiers, pronouns can cause confusion if it is not clear to what they are referring. The correction of faulty pronoun reference depends on what kind of fault is involved.

Faulty Pronoun Reference Because of the Omission of the Antecedent

When the antecedent of a pronoun is omitted, the faulty reference can be corrected by putting the antecedent back into its sentence; by substituting the antecedent for the pronoun; or by rewriting the sentence or sentences.

IMPLIED REFERENCE: Instead of setting a total fee, the orthodontist charged twenty dollars month until the work was completed, *which* the dental profession considers unethical.

CLEAR: Instead of setting a total fee, the orthodontist charged twenty dollars a month until the work was completed, *an arrangement which* the dental profession considers unethical.

(antecedent *an arrangement* stated explicitly)

IMPLIED REFERENCE: My father wants me to be a doctor, but *this* is a profession that does not appeal to me.

CLEAR: My father wants me to be a doctor, but *medicine* is a profession that does not appeal to me.
(antecedent *medicine* replacing its pronoun)

IMPLIED REFERENCE: I have visited Benson College, but I do not want to go there because *they* are snobs.

CLEAR: On my visit to Benson College, I soon found out that the students are snobs. That's why I do not want to go there. (rewrite)

Faulty Pronoun Reference Because of Reference to More Than One Possible Antecedent

When a pronoun refers to more than one antecedent, the reference is ambiguous. The ambiguous reference can be corrected by placing the pronoun close to its antecedent or by rewriting the sentence or sentences.

AMBIGUOUS: *Everybody* could see that he was a handsome little *boy* who looked closely.

CLEAR: *Everybody who* looked closely could see that he was a handsome little boy.
(pronoun placed close to its antecedent)

CLEAR: An observant person could see that he was a handsome little boy. (rewrite)

AMBIGUOUS: *The doctor* told *him* that *he* ought to take a vacation.

CLEAR: The doctor said to him, "I really ought to take a vacation." (rewrite)

CLEAR: The doctor advised the patient to take a vacation. (rewrite)

Faulty Pronoun Reference Because of Undue Separation of Antecedent and Pronoun

If a pronoun is too widely separated from its antecedent, the reference of the pronoun may be obscured. This kind of obscurity can be corrected by substituting the antecedent for the pronoun.

OBSCURE: While bathing in the *surf* at Malibu Beach, he was knocked down and almost drowned. *It* was too strong for him.

CLEAR: While bathing in *the surf* at Malibu Beach, he was knocked down and almost drowned. *The surf* was too strong for him.

OBSCURE: When *the antecedent* of a pronoun is omitted, the faulty reference can be corrected by putting *it* back into its sentence.

CLEAR: When *the antecedent* of a pronoun is omitted, the faulty reference can be corrected by putting *the antecedent* back into its sentence.

Faulty Pronoun Reference Because of Anticipatory Reference

Anticipatory reference is a word order situation in which the pronoun in a dependent clause comes before its antecedent in the independent clause. If the sentence is short, the result is acceptable: *When I received it, the shirt was stained.*

OBSCURE: If *they* are washed gently with warm water and a mild detergent and are then wrapped in a soft, absorbent cloth and left to dry, *these orlon garments* will retain their original shape and texture.

CLEAR: If *these orlon garments* are washed . . . , *they* will retain . . .

Faulty Pronoun Reference Because of Errors of Agreement

An antecedent's control of the form of its pronoun is a strong connecting device inside and outside the sentence. If errors of agreement occur, the connection between the antecedent and its pronoun is blurred. The reader knows what is meant, but his sense of form is offended. The errors of agreement should be corrected, or the usual solutions of rewriting or substituting the antecedent for the pronoun should be employed.

BLURRED: You must keep your *silverware* out of the salty air; *they* will tarnish if you don't.

CLEAR: You must keep your *silverware* out of the salty air; *it* will tarnish if you don't.
(*Silverware* is a singular collective noun.)

BLURRED: We were stunned by the riches of *Florence*. *They* have too many museums, galleries, churches, and palaces to count.

CLEAR: We were stunned by the riches of Florence. There are too many museums, galleries, churches, and palaces to count.
(*It has too many museums* . . . is possible here, because it can stand for Florence. However, the use of *they* may mean that the writer had not Florence in mind but unspecified Florentines.)

BLURRED: *James Joyce's Dubliners* is a collection of short stories about the moral life of Dublin. *He* was a native of Dublin and knew intimately the life of the city.

CLEAR: *James Joyce's Dubliners* is a collection of short stories about the moral life of Dublin. *Joyce* was a native of Dublin and knew intimately the life of the city.

(The antecedent *Joyce* is substituted for the pronoun *he.* Strictly speaking, case is not a factor in antecedent-pronoun agreement, but we are offended by the nominative following a possessive case form.)

BLURRED: *Students* should understand that the college cannot allow registration to be completed unless full payment of fees is made at the time of registration. If paying by check, *you* should make out the check to the bursar of the college.

CLEAR: . . . If payment is made by check, the check should be made out to the bursar of the college.

(The solution here is to avoid using the pronoun altogether. The passive form of the verb allows for its deletion.)

CASE

Case denotes the relation of nouns and pronouns to other words in the sentence. There are three relationships or cases:

➤ The nominative case indicates that the noun or pronoun is used as the subject of a verb, or as an appositive to a subject noun, or as a predicate noun.

> *Mary* plays the piano.
> (nominative case, subject of the verb)

> The younger *girl, Mary,* plays the piano.
> (*Mary* is in the nominative case as the appositive to *girl.*)

> The girl playing the piano is *Mary.*
> (*Mary* is in the nominative case because it is a predicate noun used after the copulative verb *is* to refer to *girl.*)

➤ The possessive case usually indicates possession.

> I tuned *Mary's* piano.

➤ The objective case indicates that the noun or pronoun receives the action of the verb or the verbal, or that it is the object of a preposition.

> I tuned the *piano.*
> (object of *tuned*)

> Tuning the *piano* was easy.
> (object of the gerund *tuning*)

> She sat down at the *piano* to play.
> (object of the preposition *at*)

Nouns and pronouns indicate case either by their position in the sentence or by their form. Nouns retain the same form in the nominative and objective cases, but change form to indicate the possessive case: *Mary's.* The personal pronouns, except you and it, have different forms for the nominative and objective cases. All personal pronouns change form for the possessive case. *(I, my, mine, me; he, his, him; she, hers, her; you, your, yours; it, its.)*

Although speakers need not always strictly adhere to the rules of case, the writer must learn to use nouns and pronouns in their proper case. Nouns cause little trouble because they change form only in the possessive case. The personal pronouns, however, cause some writers considerable difficulty and must therefore be used with special care.

Put the Subject of a Verb in the Nominative Case

John is growing taller.

He was born in Vernal, Colorado.

They are studying nuclear physics.

Put the Predicate Noun or Pronoun in the Nominative Case

The predicate noun or pronoun stands for the same person or thing as the subject and renames it. Therefore the predicate noun or pronoun is in the same case as the subject, the nominative case.

Mr. Dill is a *sexton.*

It was *he* who wrote the letter.

They thought that the thief was *I.*

Put the Appositive of a Subject in the Nominative Case

Mr. Daly, my *neighbor,* is a probation officer.

The sponsors, *we who are present here,* must sign the petition.

Put the Object of a Verb in the Objective Case

He blew the *whistle.*

We thanked *him* for his kindness.

He taught *her* Greek.

Put the Object or Complement of a Verbal in the Objective Case

Smelling the *coffee,* I jumped out of bed.
(*Coffee* is the object of the participle *smelling.*)

Whipping *him* does no good.
(*Him* is the object of the gerund *whipping.*)

I should like to be *him.*
(*Him is* the predicate complement of the infinitive *to be.*)

Put the Subject of an Infinitive in the Objective Case

We asked *him* to be our representative.
(*Him* is the subject of the infinitive *to be.*)

We hired her to demonstrate our products.
(*Her* is the subject of the infinitive *to demonstrate.*)

Put Coordinate Nouns and Pronouns in the Same Case

Mr. Sahn and *I* are on the nominating committee.
(*Mr. Sahn* and *I* are subjects of the verb and are therefore in the nominative case.)

He reported *Jones* and *me* to the supervisor.
(As objects of *reported, Jones* and *me* are in the objective case.)

In All Elliptical Clauses Introduced by *Than* and *As* Put Nouns and Pronouns in the Case that the Expanded Clause Would Demand

He received the appointment because he has more experience than *I* (*have*).

Mr. Anderson did not recommend him as highly as (he recommended) *me*.

Put the Object of a Preposition in the Objective Case

Grandmother's linens will be divided between *you* and *me*.
(*You* and *me* are objects of the preposition *between*.)

We will divide the spoils among *us*.
(*Us* is the object of the preposition *among*.)

Put the Relative Pronoun *Who* or *Whom* in the Case Demanded by Its Use in the Clause to Which It Belongs

Livingston was the man *who* was sent to find Stanley.
(*Who* introduces the dependent clause and is in the nominative case because it is the subject of the verb *was sent*.)

Who do you suppose gave him our address?
(*Who* is the subject of *gave,* not the object of the
parenthetical clause *do you suppose.*)

Whom were they talking about?
(*Whom* is the object of the preposition *about.*)

Whom do you take them to be?
(*Whom* is the complement of the infinitive *to be.*)

Help *whoever* deserves help.
(*Whoever* is the subject of the verb *deserves* and is
therefore in the nominative case.)

Put Nouns and Pronouns in the Possessive Case When They Are Used to Show the Following

➤ Possession

Carol's store
(the store that Carol owns)

his kite

➤ Connection

China's apologists
(apologists who represent China)

the bureau's legal advisors

➤ The performer of an act

Houdini's escape

the King's abdication

➤ Time, measurement, value

a day's wages
(the wages earned in a day)

a snail's pace
(the slow pace of a snail)

a dollar's worth of candy
(the amount of candy evaluated as a dollar)

Put a Noun or Pronoun in the Possessive Case When It *Immediately* Precedes a Gerund

Whenever she thinks of *Henry's leaving,* she begins to cry.

I will not take the blame for *somebody's pilfering.*

The dog ran away without *anyone's noticing* him.
(Compare this illustration with the next.)

The dog ran away without *anyone* in the house *noticing* him.
(Here the possessive case of *anyone* is not used because it does not *immediately* precede the gerund.)

NOTE: A noun preceding a participle is not in the possessive case.

The *girl singing* to the baby is my sister.
(*Singing to the baby* is a participial phrase used as an adjective to modify *girl,* the subject of the verb *is.*)

The *girl's singing* woke the baby.
(*Singing* is a gerund, the subject of the verb *woke.* The possessive case is used because the noun *girl* immediately precedes the gerund *painting.*)

DANGLING MODIFIERS

A dangling modifier is a dependent structure that is related to the wrong word in the sentence. It is usually caused by the writer's starting a construction and forgetting where he or she is going. As a result, the sentence is momentarily misleading and often ludicrous.

> **Coming around the bend in the road,* the church was seen.

In the preceding sentence, the church seems to be coming around the bend, an unusual occupation for an ecclesiastical building. The error is caused by the writer's chopping from the sentence the person who did both the seeing and the coming. The sentence can be repaired by including that person.

> *Coming around the bend in the road,* **he** saw the church.

Dangling Modifiers Involving Verbals

Most dangling modifiers involve verbals. One way of "undangling" these modifiers is to determine who or what is involved in the action of the verbal and then make sure that this person or thing is in the sentence and that the modifier stands close to it. Another way to correct this error is to transform the verbal back to a finite verb.

➤ *Dangling modifiers will often occur when the structure on which the modifier is dependent has been omitted from the sentence.*

> **Looking through his field glasses,* the bird flew away.

Looking through his field glasses, **he** saw the bird fly away.

(Who looked through the field glasses? The bird? More probably **he** did. When **he** is back in the sentence, the participle phrase stands close to it.)

*To bake a delicious cake, the **eggs** and butter must be fresh.

To bake a delicious cake, **you** must use fresh butter and **eggs.**

(Do eggs and butter bake cakes? No, people generally do that. *One* and **you** are the usual words for people in general. When **you** is placed in the sentence, the infinitive phrase stands close to it.)

➤ *In some instances, the structure that should be modified is in the sentence, but the modifier, by its position, seems to modify something else.*

* *To provide maximum coverage,* you must have a comprehensive **policy.**

To provide maximum coverage, a **policy** must be comprehensive.

(The infinitive phrase stands close to **policy.** This infinitive phrase modifier is considered a verb modifier of cause. The original sentence before transformation probably went something like this: **In order that a* **policy** *provide maximum coverage, a* **policy** *must be comprehensive.*)

*The **visitors** watched the construction men at work in the excavation, *gaping in openmouthed wonder.*

Gaping in openmouthed wonder, the **visitors** watched the construction men at work in the excavation.

(Probably, neither the excavation nor the construction men were gaping in openmouthed wonder, so the participle phrase stands close to the word it modifies—**visitors.**)

The visitors watched the construction men at work in the excavation *and gaped in openmouthed wonder.*

(The verbal becomes a finite verb to resolve the problem.)

Dangling Modifiers Involving Prepositional Phrases and Verbals

Verbals embedded inside prepositional phrases can sometimes relate to the wrong structure. **Before baking a cake, the hands should be washed.* Inside the prepositional phrase, which functions as a verb modifier, the verbal is relating to the wrong structure, *the hands.* The methods of correction presented in the previous section also apply here. The prepositional phrase with its verbal is placed close to the nominal involved in the action of the verbal: *Before baking a cake,* **you** *should wash your hands;* or the verbal is transformed into a finite verb so that the prepositional phrase becomes an adverb clause modifying a verb: *Before you bake a cake, you should wash your hands.*

*On examining his account, the discrepancy became apparent.

On examining his account, **he** discovered the discrepancy.

(*Examining* relates to **he,** while the prepositional phrase *on examining his account* modifies the verb *discovered.*)

When he examined his account, he discovered the discrepancy.

(The adverb clause *when he examined his account* modifies the verb *discovered*.)

*After beating the eggs, it is time to add the butter.

After beating the eggs, **you** should now add the butter.

After you have beaten the eggs, you should add the butter.

Dangling Modifiers Involving Elliptical Clauses

Elliptical clauses are clauses from which words have been deleted: *when she was eight years old* becomes *when eight years old.* A dangling elliptical clause is one which invites the reader to complete the elliptical clause by putting back the wrong set of words. In the following sentence, the reader is tempted to believe that the father was eight years old. **When eight years old, her father began to teach her Greek.*

The dangling modifier can be corrected by expanding the clause to recover the deleted words. *When* **she was** *eight years old, her father began to teach her Greek.* Another correction is to leave the elliptical clause as it is but make sure that the nominal *she,* which was deleted, stands close to the clause elsewhere in the sentence. *When eight years old,* **she** *was taught beginning Greek by her father.*

*When thoroughly cleaned, you should wash and salt the fish.

When the **fish has been** *thoroughly cleaned,* it should be washed and salted.

When thoroughly cleaned, the **fish** should be washed and salted.

*While reaching for the salt, his water glass fell over.

*While **he was** reaching for the salt,* his water glass fell over.

(a coincidence on a rocking railroad dining car?)

While reaching for the salt, **he** knocked over his water glass.

Generalized Participle Phrases

Some participle phrases have such a wide reference that they do not need a nominal to refer to. We do not care who is speaking in *Speaking of taxes, in our state taxes have multiplied in the last four years.* In some instances, the participle has lost its sense of action. It is doubtful if anyone is considering in *Considering the large amount of advertising, the increase in sales has been disappointing.* Certainly, nobody is owing in *Owing to certain technical difficulties, the program announced for this time will not be broadcast.*

In fact, words and phrases like *speaking of, considering, owing to, allowing, granting, assuming, according to, relating to,* and *concerning* function as prepositions and are therefore not regarded as dangling modifiers.

Some of these participles can function as true verbals, and care must be taken to distinguish their two functions.

Granting his weakened condition, he can and must be moved today.

(prepositional phrase)

Their leader, *granting Caesar's request,* allowed him to join their festivities.
(participle phrase modifying *leader*)

MISPLACED MODIFIERS

Because word order in English is very important to the functioning of structures, a modifier that gets out of position can cause confusion. A misplaced modifier usually gets that way because too often we write things down in the order in which they entered our minds. The resulting disorder can produce alarming results. Many a joke has been built around the misplacing of modifiers. *For Sale: 1988 Volkswagen by elderly gentleman recently rebored and new battery installed.* Obviously, it is the Volkswagen and not the elderly gentleman that has been modified by the reboring and battery installation. The solution, then, is to reorder the sentence so that the modifiers clearly modify the right structure. *For Sale by elderly gentleman: 1988 Volkswagen, recently rebored and new battery installed.*

Misplaced Verb Modifiers

Most verb modifiers can move around with some freedom within a sentence. This freedom can too easily become confusion because a verb modifier can attach itself to the wrong verb or noun. The solution is to bring it back close to its verb.

AMBIGUOUS: Jack threatened to divorce her *often.*

CLEAR: Jack *often* threatened to divorce her.

AMBIGUOUS: He offered to paint the fence *last night.*
(outdoor late evening painting?)

CLEAR: *Last night* he offered to paint the fence.

Misplaced Noun Modifiers

Noun modifiers have fixed positions before and after the noun. If for any reason, they are dislodged from their correct positions, confusion and ambiguity result. The sentence must be rearranged to get the noun modifier back into its correct position, or the sentence must be recast.

AMBIGUOUS: He finally got rid of his hiccups by holding his breath *which had lasted an hour.*

CLEAR: By holding his breath, he finally got rid of his hiccups *which had lasted an hour.*

CLEAR: He held his breath and stopped his hour-long bout of hiccups.

AMBIGUOUS: He shouted at the bus driver *trembling with rage.* (two angry drivers?)

CLEAR: *Trembling with rage,* he shouted at the bus driver.

Noun modifiers that are prepositional phrases can give particular trouble because if they are misplaced, they not only can refer to other nouns, but they also can become verb modifiers on the spot. In the following ambiguous sentence, it is impossible to tell who, if anybody, is inside that refrigerated showcase.

*Ginny showed the rare orchids to the customer *in the refrigerated showcase.*

Double Reference Modifiers

Some structures are so placed that they can refer to the structure before or the structure after them. These squinting modifiers are sometimes completely ambiguous. The use of punctuation to separate the modifier from one of the structures sometimes helps, but it is better to move the squinting modifier to a position where it will look in one direction only.

AMBIGUOUS: The doctor said that if my aunt did not move to a warmer climate *within a year* she would be dead.
(Must she move within a year, or will she be dead within a year?)

CLEAR: The doctor said that if my aunt did not move to a warmer climate she would dead *within a year.*

AMBIGUOUS: While we were dining in Flagstaff, Arizona, *on the advice of a fellow traveler* we decided to see Boulder Dam.
(The comma does make the prepositional phrase refer more to Boulder Dam than to dining in Flagstaff, but it is still not clear.)

CLEAR: While we were dining in Flagstaff, Arizona, we decided, *on the advice of a fellow traveler, to* see Boulder Dam.

Misplaced Common Adverbs

In colloquial speech, adverbs like *only, almost, merely, scarcely, just,* and *even* are often misplaced without unduly confusing the listener. Luigi *only had $20 with him at the time* is clear in its meaning. In formal writing, however, these adverbs should be placed next to the structures they modify. *Luigi had only $20 . . .*

COLLOQUIAL: He *merely* asked the question because he was curious.

FORMAL: He asked the question *merely* because he was curious.

COLLOQUIAL: She *almost* washed all the dishes. (This sentence is not totally clear; it could that she thought about it but watched television instead.)

FORMAL: She washed *almost* all the dishes. (Here she did get her hands wet.)

Faulty Phrase Compounding

Faulty phrase compounding is the careless or too enthusiastic compounding of phrases. This kind of compounding involves the placing of several structures to the left of a noun or an adjective. The following is an example of phrase compounding.

A low temperature, steam-operated bronze dough- nut press
(This machine is probably a bronze press, operated by steam, which stamps out doughnuts at low temperatures. It could also be a press located in a chilly room and stamping out bronze doughnuts.)

Because compounded phrases can be vague or ambiguous and because new compounds are being invented all the time by product packagers, mind-conditioning experts, engineers, and social scientists, great care must be exercised in using these essential but often uncontrollable structures.

Below is a listing of compounded noun and adjective phrases ranging from those long-accepted to those that definitely are to be avoided. Note that the hyphen is used frequently in these compounds. When you are compounding, it is wise to have a good modern dictionary at hand.

➤ *Long-accepted, usable noun-phrase/adjective-phrase compounds*

roadside cafe: The cafe sits beside a road.

waterproof: Something is impervious to water.

baby-sitter: Someone sits with or looks after a baby. (Note that doing the same thing for an old man does not make one an old man-sitter.)

fly-by-night operation: The operation has a temporary, unreliable character. (To avoid one's creditors, one would leave town in the middle of the night.)

➤ *Acceptable, recently coined noun-phrase/adjective-phrase compounds*

dropout: Someone has dropped out of school or out of organized society.

hang-up: Something has irritated or inhibited someone so that he has become tense. (as if someone had hung him on a hook?)

war-related: Something is related to an activity connected with war-making.

| fully automated, disc-oriented computer system | A system of machines that can compute automatically is oriented to a (magnetic) disc. |

SPLIT CONSTRUCTIONS

Because word order is so vital to English, the words of a particular structure should stand together. For emphasis or clarity, a good writer will alter the expected flow of words and structures. However, the pointless separation of words within a structure or of closely related structures may cause awkwardness or obscurity. When separation produces either of these effects, the writer should change the order of the words or revise the sentence.

Pointless Separation of Words Within a Structure

The basic elements of a structure such as preposition and object or auxiliary verb and main verb can at times be separated by short intruders like *at times,* but the integrity of the structure is threatened by larger interruptions.

➤ *The verb phrase*

ACCEPTABLE: You *can* never *go* home.

AWKWARD: There stands the house that I *will*, within five years, *purchase and remodel.*

IMPROVED: There stands the house that I will *purchase and remodel* within five years.

➤ *The noun phrase*

AWKWARD: She's *a talented,* and here I must point out that I have good qualifications to make such a judgment, *intelligent person.*

IMPROVED SOMEWHAT: She is a talented person, and because I think that my qualifications are good enough to make such a judgment, I would add further that she is also an intelligent person.

➤ *The infinitive with* to

AWKWARD: I hope that you will be able *to* satisfactorily *repair* my television set within a week.

IMPROVED: I hope that you will be able *to repair* my television set satisfactorily within a week.

AWKWARD: You must begin *to*, if you have the time, *read* more widely in the literature of psychology.

IMPROVED: If you have the time, you must begin *to read* more widely in the literature of psychology.

➤ *The prepositional phrase*

AWKWARD: He pawed through every garment on the bargain counter, looking *for,* in that welter, *a short-sleeved shirt.*

IMPROVED: He pawed through every garment on the bargain counter, looking *for a short-sleeved shirt* in that welter.

Pointless Separation of Closely Related Structures

Closely related structures such as subject, verb, and verb completion, and antecedent and pronoun depend on word order and proximity to signal their relationships. They can be separated by some structures, but larger interruptions strain the fabric of the sentence.

➤ *Basic sentence elements: subject, verb, verb completion*

ACCEPTABLE: *Mean Joe Greene,* with savage intensity, *cut down* the opposing quarterback.

AWKWARD: *Mean Joe Greene,* and you'll agree when I say his name that he's one of the greatest linemen ever, *played* a great game against Dallas.

IMPROVED: *Mean Joe Greene,* one of the greatest linemen to play football, *played* a great game against Dallas. (This illustration cheats a little because the large structure separating the subject from its verb is an appositive, which technically belongs to the noun phrase dependent on *Mean Joe Greene.*)

AWKWARD: Looking through his binoculars, he *saw* on the opposite shore *a group of bathers.*

IMPROVED: Looking through his binoculars, he *saw a group of bathers* on the opposite shore.

➤ *Coordinated elements*

AWKWARD:	*The men removed their hats* when the queen appeared on the balcony *and the ladies cheered.*
IMPROVED:	*The men removed their hats and the ladies cheered* when the queen appeared on the balcony.

➤ *Antecedent and pronoun*

ACCEPTABLE:	*The cows* in the west pasture, *which* were lowing piteously, needed milking. (This separation is justified because in the fixed word order of noun phrases, the prepositional phrase must precede the adjective clause .)
AWKWARD:	He was most impressed by the *applicant,* as I fully expected, *whom* his brother-in-law recommended.
IMPROVED:	As I fully expected, he was most impressed by *the applicant whom* his in-law recommended.

Mixed Constructions

In speaking, we sometimes start one structure, slide to another structure, forget the first structure and start all over again. A written court transcript of testimony given under some pressure makes the point well.

> When I got to the door, and just as I was going down the steps, it was about seven thirty I think, well maybe seven thirty-five, I don't tell time too well, anyway I was going to get my car fixed and

> I saw this man coming up to me, he was about my
> height and he asked me where Seventh Street
> was, I think he was wearing a rain . . .

The initial adverb clauses have long been forgotten as
the witness, groping for continuity, continues to mix up
his constructions.

In writing, where we usually have the chance to
rewrite, the mixed constructions should be tracked
down and eliminated.

MIXED: There is no one *to* whom he can apply *to*
          for help. (Here *to whom* and *whom . . . to*
          have been blended. The solution is to
          omit one *to*.)

MIXED: I told him to invest in mutual funds if *he
          can.* (The direct statement present tense
          can has been left in a sentence trans-
          formed to indirect statement. The
          solutions are to undo or to complete the
          transform.)

IMPROVED: I told him, "Invest in mutual funds if *you
          can.*"

IMPROVED: I told him to invest in mutual funds if *he
          could.*

MIXED: *In order to complete the installation
          before the end of the month* is why we
          are working overtime. (The writer started
          with an infinitive phrase verb modifier,
          forgot this fact, and converted it to a
          nominal subject.)

IMPROVED: *In order to complete the installation
          before the end of the month, we* are

working overtime. (This is the sentence as first planned. The infinitive phrase is an introductory verb modifier, and the logical subject is *we*.)

IMPROVED: *To complete the installation before the end of the month* is the reason why we are working overtime. (The writer stays with the conversion of the infinitive phrase to a nominal and makes it the subject of *is*. A final improvement would be to switch the two nominals around so that the sentence started with the noun nominal, *the reason.*)

MIXED: The company repudiated the agreement *which,* although it made several concessions to the union, the terms seemed to be to its advantage. (Before one construction is completed the sentence shifts to another, leaving *which* without a finite verb.)

IMPROVED: The company repudiated the agreement *which,* although it made several concessions to the union, seemed to be to its advantage. (*Which* is now the subject of *seemed.*)

MIXED: Agencies must figure out how many people *will* the advertisement *reach.* (This is a transform where the question has not been completely embedded into the declarative sentence. The solutions are to undo the transform by returning to the direct question or to complete the

transform by changing the form of the
verb to *will reach*.)

IMPROVED: Agencies must ask themselves the
following question: how many people
will the advertisement *reach?*

IMPROVED: Agencies must figure out how many
people the advertisement *will reach.*

FAULTY COMPARISON

Mistakes are made in writing comparisons because the
meanings of the comparative and superlative forms of
the adjective pose problems and because elements of a
comparison may be wrongly omitted.

Faulty Omission of Elements from the Second Part of the Comparison

A comparison is nearly always shortened by the
deletion of repeated elements. *She is more beautiful
than* her sister (*is*) (*beautiful*). Sometimes the omission
of elements from the second half of a comparison can
be done badly so that the reader is confused by the
ambiguity involved.

The ambiguous sentence *Shaw liked Wagner better
than Verdi* has been cut back so that the reader cannot
tell whether the original comparison involved Verdi
and Shaw as appreciators of Wagner or whether it
involved Shaw's appreciation of Wagner and Verdi:
Shaw liked Wagner better than Verdi (liked) (Wagner)
or *Shaw liked Wagner better than (Shaw) (liked) Verdi.*
Here is a second example of this kind of deletion
problem.

COMPLETE COMPARISON:	Carla ranks Cole Porter higher than Carla ranks Barry Manilow.
FAULTY OMISSION:	*Carla ranks Cole Porter higher than Barry Manilow. (Manilow has become an evaluator of Cole Porter.)
COMPARISON RESTORED:	Carla ranks Cole Porter higher than she ranks Barry Manilow.

Omission of the Basis of Comparison

Comparisons should not be approximate. Things being compared should be stated precisely. In the following example, a fuzzy comparison is made between states and mountains.

> *The mountains in Vermont are lower and greener than New Hampshire.

> The mountains in Vermont are lower and greener than the *mountains* in New Hampshire.
> (Mountains are now correctly compared to mountains.)

> OR

> The mountains in Vermont are lower and greener than *those* in New Hampshire.

Omission of *As* in Double Comparisons

Both *as* and *than* are involved where a comparison is made twice.

> In the ring, Tag Martin is as ferocious *as,* if not more ferocious *than,* Mike Tyson.

Because the structure looks formidable, a writer will often omit the first comparison word *as*.

> *In the ring, Tag Martin is as ferocious, if not more ferocious, *than* Mike Tyson.

The easiest correction is to avoid the structure altogether and write something with roughly the same meaning. *In the ring, Tag Martin is at least as ferocious as Mike Tyson.* If the double comparison seems essential, the solution is to separate the two comparisons and delete the second comparison word *than*.

> In the ring, Tag Martin is as ferocious *as* Mike Tyson, if not more ferocious.

Confusion of the Normal Meanings of the Comparative and Superlative Forms

The rule is that the comparative form refers to two things; the superlative form refers to more than two things. In speech and colloquial writing, however, the superlative sometimes does the job of the comparative form: *She was certainly the tallest of the twins.* In formal writing, the distinctions between the two forms must be kept. *She is the taller of the twins. I am the oldest of three brothers* (not *I am the older of three brothers*).

Confusion of the Meanings of Comparative and Superlative Forms by Misuse of the Word *Other*

The meaning of the comparative form of the adjective, where an individual is *singled out* to be compared to other members of its group, is made explicit by the use of the word **other.** If this word is omitted, the result can be confusing.

CONFUSING: Alaska is bigger than any state in the union. (This comparison implies that Alaska is *not* a state in the union.)

CLEAR: Alaska is bigger than any **other** state in the union.

CONFUSING: Charlie is older than any boy in the class. (Charlie is not a boy?)

CLEAR: Charlie is older than any **other** boy in the class.

The superlative form of the adjective is used when an individual is included within the members of the group which are being compared to the individual. When the individual is included in the group, the excluding word **other** should not be used.

CONFUSING: Charlie is the oldest of all the **other** boys in the class. (*All* includes Charlie; *other* excludes Charlie.)

CLEAR: Charlie is the oldest of all the boys in the class.

OMISSION OF NECESSARY WORDS

If structures are not unduly separated and each structure is well constructed, writers will frequently delete words when they feel confident that the construction of the parts of a sentence is clear. When an instruction pamphlet has in it the elliptical structure *when assembling the case for the clock,* we know that words like *you are* have been omitted from the adverb clause *when you are assembling the case of the clock.*

We are expected to fill in the gaps and we do (fill in the gaps). In *He had been tried and judged already,* we supply the *had been* for the second verb. Even when the verb form is not repeated, we can be trusted to think of the right verb form. In the sentence *His manner was offensive, his reasons lame,* the deleted verb form is not *was* but *were.* Some people do object to the lack of repetition because it offends their sense of form, but the meaning is clear.

Because the deletion of words can cause awkwardness and misunderstanding, care must be taken in handling these deletions. There are times when our sense of form is offended; there are times when we have to work to fill in the gaps. Below are listed some of the many situations where it is wise not to delete words from their structures.

Omission of Necessary Determiners in Coordinate Forms

AMBIGUOUS: When he appeared for the hearing he was accompanied by a friend and advisor. (one or two people?)

CLEAR: When he appeared for the hearing he was accompanied by a friend and *an* advisor. (two people)

CLEAR: When he appeared for the hearing he was accompanied by Jack Lipsky, a friend and advisor. (one person)

AMBIGUOUS: From his income tax he deducted the expenses for his office and showroom. (two places or one place?)

CLEAR: From his income tax he deducted the expenses for his office and *his* showroom. (two places)

Omission of Necessary Prepositions

COMPLETE: From his income tax he deducted the expenses for his office and *for* his showroom. (Our sense of form approves the parallelism.)

INCOMPLETE: He has never expressed trust or loyalty to anyone.

COMPLETE: He has never expressed trust *in* or loyalty to anyone. (It is clear what is meant without the preposition *in*. However, we habitually associate certain prepositions with certain nouns and adjectives. Thus our sense of form is pleased by the contrast of *in* and *to*.)

INCOMPLETE: It is either similar or different from each of the preceding propositions.

COMPLETE: It is either similar *to* or different from each of the preceding propositions.

Omission of Repeated Verb Forms in Coordinate but Not Parallel Verb Phrases

INCOMPLETE: He had laughed and been reprimanded for his action.

COMPLETE: He had laughed and *had* been reprimanded for his action.

INCOMPLETE: He was late for work and
reprimanded by the supervisor.

COMPLETE: He was late for work and *was*
reprimanded by the supervisor.

Omission of Relationship Words and Other Small Words

TELEGRAPHIC: Reported late to work this morning
because of minor accident. Slightly
stunned by chilly reception from
outer office, warmed by inner
sanctum's ho-hum attitude.

IMPROVED: *I* reported late to work this morning
because of *a* minor accident. *I was*
slightly stunned by *the* chilly
reception from *the* outer office;
however, I was warmed by *the* inner
sanctum's ho-hum attitude.

The telegraphic style should be kept for private papers
such as letters, diaries, class notes and telegrams.

Chapter 5

Emphasis, Consistency, and Appropriateness

EMPHASIS

It is frequently desirable to emphasize an entire sentence, or a single word or a group of words within a sentence. Without the use of emphasis, writing is flat and uninteresting.

Emphasis by Arrangement

To give prominence to an entire sentence, place it at either the beginning or end of the paragraph. The beginning of a paragraph calls attention to itself simply because it is the first thing to engage the reader's attention. The end of a paragraph can be made prominent by building the previous sentences to a climax, or by arranging them in an order of ascending importance so that the thought expressed by the concluding sentence is given added forcefulness by what precedes it.

> The roads were hot and dusty. The grass in the meadows was burned to a parched golden brown. Cattle in dried-up river bottoms licked hopefully at gravel and rocks where water had always been before. *It had not rained for weeks, and there would be no rain for two more weeks to come.*

To give emphasis to single words or groups of words, pay attention to the arrangement of the order of the words as they occur in the sentence. Words at the beginning and end of a sentence are likely to attract more attention than words in the middle. Words or phrases placed out of their usual or expected positions also call attention to themselves. Careful use of these general principles—avoiding the abuse of straining too hard or too frequently for special effects—is a large part of the secret of varied and effective writing.

In normal English word order, for example, adjectives precede the nouns they modify. Reversing this order calls particular attention to the adjectives.

> NORMAL: The *tired old* judge slumped on the bench.

> REVERSED: The judge, *old* and *tired,* slumped on the bench.

This procedure cannot be used for a single adjective without producing an overly artificial effect: *The judge, old, slumped on the bench.*

In normal word order the flow of a sentence moves from the subject to the verb and concludes with words related to the verb (as verb completions or modifiers).

The captain led his men into battle.
(object *men* and modifier *into battle*)

The young man walked *rapidly down the street because he was anxious to get home.*
(adverbial modifiers after verb)

The only exception occurs when the sentence is introduced by the expletive *it* or *there: There were forty men in the room.*

The following sentence represents the usual flow of words:

John and Barbara were married on a sunny afternoon in late
November.

(subject)　　　　　(verb)　　　(adverbial modifiers)

The statement is clear, but no part of it is emphasized because the order of the words is exactly what the reader expects. To give prominence to adverbial modifiers, place them at the beginning of the sentence. To emphasize the date, recast the sentence to read:

In late November, John and Barbara were married
on a sunny afternoon.

To emphasize both the weather and the date, revise the sentence to read:

On a sunny afternoon in late November, John and
Barbara were married.

Observe particularly how placing the adverbial modifiers (on *a sunny afternoon in late November*) at the beginning of the sentence not only makes them more prominent but also gives greater emphasis to the concluding verb *were married*. Notice, too, how the abnormal word order of this sentence calls attention to the entire sentence and makes it more interesting and emphatic.

The same principle applies to the position of single words in the sentence.

NORMAL:　He drew himself to attention
　　　　　smartly.

EMPHATIC:　Smartly he drew himself to
　　　　　attention.

To give emphasis to the object of a verb (which normally follows the verb), place the object at the beginning of the sentence.

> NORMAL: They made him president.

> EMPHATIC: Him they made president.

In some sentences, a telling and dramatic effect can be achieved by completely reversing normal word order.

> NORMAL: The soldiers marched into the battle.

> REVERSED: Into the battle marched the soldiers.

CAUTION: Do not try to recast every sentence, or even the majority of sentences, to secure emphasis. Such a procedure defeats its own purpose by producing an effect of strained and artificial writing. In the following paragraph, the plight of three boys is described. The writer was principally interested in one of the boys, John. He therefore reserves the description of John's misfortune for the end, and he uses abnormal word order only in the concluding sentence.

> They tied Fred to a tree. They perched Jimmy on top of a high rock. John they threw into the river.

Observe how the beginning and end of a sentence call attention to themselves, particularly when the word order is at all unusual. It follows that, even in the construction of ordinary sentences, it is foolish to place unimportant words or phrases in emphatic positions. In the sentence,

> However, the nurse did not arrive.

the sentence modifier *however* does not deserve the emphasis its position gives it. Revising the sentence to

> The nurse, however, did not arrive.

gives prominence to the essential parts of the statement.

Similarly, unimportant words or phrases at the end of a sentence occupy a position of prominence that would be better held by more important material.

> Thousands of spectators packed the stadium to watch the championship game on Thanksgiving Day.

Unless the date is important in this sentence, it should be inserted within the sentence:

> Thousands of spectators packed the stadium on Thanksgiving Day tot watch the championship game.

Emphasis by Repetition

When a word or phrase is repeated immediately or soon after its original use, the reader is certain to notice the repetition. Deliberate repetition is one method of obtaining emphasis.

> His father was *weak,* his sister was *weak,* and he was *weak.*

> . . . that government of the *people,* by the *people,* for the *people* . . .

Note the use of repetition in the following brief narrative.

> "Houses of refuge *don't have crews,*" said the correspondent. "As I understand them, they are

only places where clothes and grub are stored for the benefit of shipwrecked people. They don't carry crews."

"Oh, yes, they do," said the cook.

"No, they don't," said the correspondent.

"Well, *we're not there yet,* anyhow," *said the oiler in the stern.*

"Well," said the cook, "perhaps it's not a house of refuge that I'm thinking of as being near Mosquito Inlet Light. Perhaps it's a life-saving station."

"We're not there yet," said the oiler in the stern.

—Stephen Crane, "The Open Boat"

Emphasis by Use of Voice

The choice of active or passive voice should depend on which element of the sentence is to be emphasized. In a typical sentence containing a transitive verb, such as

John *owns* a horse.

the use of the active voice emphasizes John's ownership. If the statement is intended to answer a question about the horse, it should be placed in the passive voice:

The horse *is owned* by John.

In general, if there is no particular problem of emphasis, the active voice is preferable since it is more direct and gives a stronger effect.

The members *will be notified* by the president.

is less emphatic than

The president will notify the members.

Emphasis by Subordination

To give a flat and lifeless effect to writing, the simplest device is to use only simple and compound sentences in normal word order. Writers often do this deliberately to create a pallid atmosphere:

> He went into the house. He looked around listlessly for a few minutes and then slumped into a chair. No sound was heard except the ticking of the clock. He rested his head on the back of the chair and gradually fell into a deep and profound sleep.

But to indicate distinctions between ideas of greater and lesser importance, place the lesser words and phrases in subordinate positions in the sentence and the less important clauses in the subordinate form. In the following sentence, nothing is emphasized, and the entire statement is flat:

> New York City is on the East Coast, and it is America's largest seaport.

To stress the location of New York City, recast the sentence as follows:

> New York City, which is America's largest seaport, is on the East Coast.

To stress the importance of New York City as a seaport, rewrite the sentence:

> New York City, which is on the East Coast, is America's largest seaport.

Coordination and Balance

Words and phrases are coordinated by using the co-ordinating conjunctions *and, but, or, nor, for,* and *yet.*

He was poor *but* happy.

The decor of the lobby was rich, *yet* unobtrusive.

Clauses are coordinated by joining them with a coordinating conjunction or a semicolon.

Ideas of equal importance are given equal prominence by coordination. The elements to be coordinated are given increased emphasis if they are balanced: presented in approximately the same number of words, the same kind of words, and in identical or closely similar word order.

He gained great wealth, but he lost his honor.

To err is human; to forgive, divine.

Years ago, the man was the hunter; the woman was the cook.

She'll come willingly, or she won't come at all.

Balance also gives effectiveness to simple assertions:

Sauce for the goose is sauce for the gander.

Over the fence is out of bounds.

Parallelism and Balance

Two or more ideas that are similar in nature are known as parallel ideas. For effective presentation, express them in parallel form: a noun should be paralleled with a noun, an infinitive with an infinitive, a subordinate clause with another subordinate clause, and so on.

PARALLEL NOUNS: They studied *history, mathematics,* and *chemistry.*

NOT PARALLEL: They studied about the past, mathematics, and how matter is constituted.

PARALLEL INFINITIVES:	He learned *to swim, to play* tennis, and *to ride* a horse.
NOT PARALLEL:	He learned to play tennis, swimming, and the art of horseback riding.
PARALLEL CLAUSES:	In her praises of the summer camp, she mentioned *that the food was good, that the climate was perfect,* and *that the equipment was superb.*
NOT PARALLEL:	In her praises of the summer camp, she mentioned the good food, that the climate was perfect, and what superb equipment they had.
PARALLEL PARTICIPLES:	The old house was *battered* by the rain and *bleached* by the sun.
NOT PARALLEL:	The old house was battered by the rain and there was no color left because it was standing in the open sunlight.

If possible, balance parallel ideas by expressing them in approximately the same number of words, the same kind of words, and in identical or closely similar word order.

NEITHER PARALLEL NOR BALANCED:	He was a good merchant, but was very poor at keeping books.
PARALLEL AND BALANCED:	He was a *good merchant,* but a *poor bookkeeper.*

NEITHER PARALLEL NOR BALANCED:	He believed in democracy for the upper classes, but felt that the common people should be ruled by their superiors.
PARALLEL AND BALANCED:	He believed in *democracy for the powerful,* but *autocracy for the weak.*
PARALLEL AND BALANCED:	It *is* wiser *to invest than to squander,* to *seek out friends than to collect acquaintances, to treasure life than to throw it away.*

Notice how parallelism, balance, and repetition are combined in the following celebrated passage from I Corinthians 13:

Though I speak with the tongues of men and of angels, and have not charity, I am become as sounding brass, or a tinkling cymbal. And though I have the gift of prophecy, and understand all mysteries, and all knowledge; and though I have all faith, so that I could remove mountains, and have not charity, I am nothing. And though I bestow all my goods to feed the poor, and though I give my body to be burned, and have not charity, it profiteth me nothing.

Charity suffereth long, and is kind; charity envieth not; charity vaunteth not itself, is not puffed up, doth not behave itself unseemly, seeketh not her own, is not easily provoked, thinketh no evil; rejoiceth not in iniquity, but rejoiceth in the truth; beareth all things, believeth all things, hopeth all things, endureth all things.

Charity never faileth: but whether there be prophecies, they shall fail; whether there be tongues, they shall cease; whether there be knowledge, it shall vanish away. For we know in part, and we prophesy in part. But when that which is perfect is come, then that which is in part shall be done away.

When I was a child, I spake as a child, I understood as a child, I thought as a child: but when I became a man, I put away childish things. For now we see through a glass, darkly; but then face to face; now I know in part; but then shall I know even as also I am known. And now abideth faith, hope, charity, these three; but the greatest of these is charity.

CONSISTENCY

In dealing with any subject, decide in advance on the method of treating the subject. Then endeavor to be consistent, avoiding such departures from the selected method as might creep in through carelessness or forgetfulness.

Consistency in Tense

When writing a narrative, decide on a basic tense and do not change it unless the reference to some prior or subsequent event demands a change.

INCONSISTENT: John *sprang* to his feet when he *heard* the whistle. He *ran* as fast as he could to reach the upper deck. There he *sees* a battleship bearing down on them. He *would remember* that moment for years to come.
(Consistent because the reference is to the future)

Consistency in Number

When discussing a type or a class, decide in advance whether to use the singular or plural number and do not change it.

INCONSISTENT: The automatic washing *machine* is a great invention. *It* saves *home-makers* many hours of drudgery. *These machines* are among the most wonderful inventions of the twentieth century.

CONSISTENT: The automatic washing *machine* is a great *invention. It* saves the *homemaker* many hours of drudg-ery. This *machine* is *one* of the most wonderful inventions of the twentieth century.

Consistency in Person

Decide in advance whether a piece of writing is to be personal or impersonal, and do not change the point of view.

INCONSISTENT: When learning to play a piano, *the student* should remember that great care and precision are essential. You should practice simple pieces until they are completely mastered. *One* can never succeed in an art if the fundamentals are neglected.

In this paragraph, either the *You* in the second sentence should be changed to *He or she* or the entire paragraph should be written as a direct appeal to the reader, as:

When learning to play a piano, remember that great care and precision are essential. You should practice simple pieces until they are completely mastered. You can never succeed in an art if you neglect the fundamentals.

Consistency and Appropriateness in Tone

Unless you wish to jar the reader by some sudden intrusion, keep the tone and level of writing constant. Informal or chatty writing admits the use of slang or colloquialisms which are out of keeping with formal writing. The appropriateness of words in given contexts is learned only by reading and listening. But notice the absurdity of the following:

> The dean exhorted the statutory members of the faculty to redouble their efforts and *get going*.

> I get sick and tired of hearing you squawk about your *lassitude*.

> Fourscore and seven years ago, our fathers brought forth on this continent a new nation, conceived in liberty, and dedicated to the proposition that *CEOs are no better than street burger-flippers*.

There are many synonyms in the English language which, although nearly identical in meaning, are appropriately used only in certain connections. The word *love* means *zero,* but only in the game of tennis. *Tip, gratuity, and perquisite* all mean some kind of value received as incidental and variable rather than as fixed income. In normal usage, however, the word *tip*—technically an acronym meaning "To Insure

Prompt Service"—is connected with frequent small amounts of money for trivial services, *gratuity* with a considerable sum of money in reward for lengthy service, *and perquisite* with certain emoluments or values that accompany political offices and some professions. Similarly, *salary, pay, wage, fee,* and *honorarium* are roughly synonymous, but are applicable to different types and levels of monetary remuneration. Also, we say that a lawyer is *retained,* a laborer is *hired,* a minister is *called,* a clerk is *employed,* and a physician is *consulted.*

Be observant of word usage in your reading. When consulting a dictionary, read the entire entry, not just one of the definitions, to get as much of a sense of the word as possible.

VARIETY

The sentence structure appropriate to a given piece of writing depends on the nature of the subject, the purpose of the author, and the anticipated audience. Directions, for example, should be written in simple language and short sentences.

To reach the Denby Road Church:

1. Follow Route 4 to Carmine Street.

2. Turn right and continue to the second traffic signal (Denby Road).

3. Turn left on Denby Road.

4. You will see the church on the right hand side of the street.

Short, direct sentences are also effective in describing action:

> A succession of loud and shrill screams, bursting
> suddenly from the throat of the chained form,
> seemed to thrust me violently back. For a brief
> moment I hesitated—I trembled. Unsheathing my
> rapier, I began to grope with it about the recess; but
> the thought of an instant reassured me. I placed my
> hand upon the solid fabric of the catacombs, and
> felt satisfied. I reapproached the wall. I replied to
> the yells of him who clamored. I reechoed—
> I aided—I surpassed them in volume and in
> strength. I did this, and the clamorer grew still.
>
> —Edgar Allan Poe, "The Cask of Amontillado"

In other kinds of writing where no special effect is
sought for, avoid monotony by varying the lengths of
sentences and by avoiding a series of sentences with
nearly identical structure and word order, such as occur
in the following example:

> When I was a boy, my comrades and I had only one
> permanent ambition: to be steamboatmen. Although
> we had transient ambitions of other sorts, they were
> only transient. When a circus came and went, it left
> us all burning to become clowns. When the first
> negro minstrel show came to town, we all wanted to
> try that kind of life. Every once in a while, we all had
> the ambition to become pirates. Although all of
> these ambitions gradually faded out, the ambition to
> be steamboatmen always remained.

Essentially the same material is given variety and
interest by sentences of varied length and structure in
Mark Twain's *Life on the Mississippi:*

When I was a boy, there was but one permanent ambition among my comrades in our village on the west bank of the Mississippi River. That was, to be a steamboatman. We had transient ambitions of other sorts, but they were only transient. When a circus came and went, it left us all burning to become clowns; the first minstrel show that ever came to our section left us all suffering to try that kind of life; now and then we had a hope that, if we lived and were good, God would permit us to be pirates. These ambitions faded out, each in its turn; but the ambition to be a steamboatman always remained .

In the following selection, the opening of William Hazlitt's essay *On Familiar Style,* notice how the first short, direct sentence attracts attention. Then notice the varied length of the second, third, and fourth sentences, which are followed by an effective parallelism in the fifth sentence. The sixth sentence, quite long, acts as a kind of summation.

[1.] It is not easy to write a familiar style. [2.] Many people mistake a familiar for a vulgar style, and suppose that to write without affectation is to write at random. [3.] On the contrary, there is nothing that requires more precision, and, if I may say so, purity of expression, than the style I am speaking of. [4.] It utterly rejects not only all unmeaning pomp, but all low, cant phrases, and loose, unconnected, slip-shod allusions. [5.] It is not to take the first word that offers, but the best word in common use; it is not to throw words together in any combinations we please, but to follow and avail ourselves of the true idiom of the language. [6.] To write a genuine familiar or truly English style, is to write as any one would speak in common conversation, who had a thorough command and choice of words, or who could discourse with ease, force, and perspicuity, setting aside all pedantic and oratorical flourishes.

Chapter 6
Punctuation

Punctuation is a device used to assist the reader. It takes the place of changes in tone, inflection, and volume, and of pauses and facial expressions, by which a speaker clarifies meaning.

TERMINAL PUNCTUATION
The Period
The principal use of the period is to indicate the end of a sentence that is not a question or an exclamation.

> The president was elected.   (statement)
>
> I asked if he would see me.   (indirect question)
>
> Please shut the door.   (request or command)

The period is often used for terminal purposes when a sentence is not involved, as after numbers in a list:

1. The President

2. The Council

3. The Board of Trustees

The period is used to terminate most abbreviations:

> e.g., i.e., Mr., Dr., Rev., etc.

Three periods are used to indicate the omission of one or more words or even sentences in a quotation:

> "I pledge allegiance . . . to the republic . . ."

When the omission occurs after the end of a sentence, the three periods are added after the period which terminates the sentence:

"Shakespeare was born in 1564. . . . He married Anne Hathaway in 1582."

The Question Mark

The question mark is used to terminate a direct question of any sort:

Who are you? Why? Why not? He did?

When enclosed in parentheses, the question mark indicates uncertainty or doubt:

He lived from 1635 (?) to 1680.

The Exclamation Point

Use the exclamation point to terminate a strong expression of feeling. Do not use it for indications of mild emotion.

Nonsense! I don't believe you.

I'll shoot the first man who moves!

Get out of this house at once!

Be sparing in the use of exclamations. The effectiveness of exclamation points is dulled by overuse.

THE COMMA

The comma is the most frequently used (and abused) aid to reading. Most poor users of commas annoy their readers by inserting illogical commas or too many commas. There is no need for uncertainty if the basic principles governing the use of the comma are clearly understood.

To Separate Parts of a Series

Use the comma to separate words, phrases, or clauses in a series. It is a substitute for a coordinating conjunction.

> John, Fred, Harry, Frank
> (John and Fred and Harry and Frank)

Usually the final element in the series is preceded by *and* or *or* to indicate the nature and the termination of the series.

> John, Fred, Harry, and Frank

A comma before the terminating conjunction (*and* or *or*), although not absolutely essential, is used to prevent confusion because of the not infrequent appearance of *and* within the members of a series:

> She shopped at Johnson's, Ward and Nelson's, and French's.

> He ate soup, meat and potatoes, and pie.

> He went across the sidewalk, down the street, and into the bar and grill.

> She asked to see the manager, she complained about the merchandise and the service, and she got satisfaction.

A single adjectival modifying a noun is frequently so necessary that it may be considered a part of the identification: *pine* tree, *drinking* glass, *red* dress. Another adjective preceding such an adjective-noun phrase functions as if it modified the entire phrase and is therefore not separated from the phrase by a comma: *tall* pine tree, *large* drinking glass, *beautiful* red dress.

To call attention to each adjective as individually and separately describing the noun, use a comma to separate the adjectives:

a tall, dark, distinguished gentleman

A comma between adjectivals has the same effect as the conjunction *and*.

a tall and dark and distinguished gentleman

To Separate the Clauses of a Compound Sentence Joined by a Coordinating Conjunction

Use the comma to separate the independent clauses of a compound sentence when they are joined by a coordinating conjunction. The comma is placed immediately before the conjunction (*and, but, or, not, for, yet*) to indicate that the conjunction introduces a clause.

The mayor invited the members of the committee to lunch, *and* most of them accepted her invitation.

I haven't succeeded in balancing my checkbook, *yet* I plan to continue writing checks.

When the clauses are very short so that most or all of the sentence can be taken in instantaneously by the eye, the comma is not required.

He sent for her and she came.

To Separate Interjections and Similar Nonintegrated Sentence Elements

Occasionally, words or phrases in a sentence are not integrated in the sentence structure. That is, they do not modify specific words, they are not subjects or verbs, they are not objects of prepositions, and so on. Separate such nonintegrated words or phrases from the remainder of the sentence by commas.

➤ Use the comma to set off interjections which are included in sentences.

>*Oh,* I thought so.

>*Hey,* watch your step!

>*Hello,* I'm glad to see you.

If the interjection occurs within the sentence, it is separated by two commas.

>I tried so hard, *alas,* to do it.

Use the comma to set off any other words or phrases that behave as interjections:

a. The adverbs *yes* and *no* are frequently used as interjections.

>*Yes,* I'll be glad to.

b. Terms of direct address are normally used as interjections.

>*John,* get the book.

>*You over there,* put on your hat.

➤ Use the comma to set off sentence modifiers. Words like *however, moreover, furthermore, therefore, nevertheless* and phrases like *on the other hand, in addition, to the contrary* often modify the whole sentence instead of a single word within the sentence. To make clear that they are not intended to modify a single word, separate them from the rest of the sentence by commas.

However, she caught the train.

He tried, *moreover,* to attain his goal.

On the other hand, he wasted his money.

➤ Use the comma to set off absolute phrases. An absolute phrase, made up of a noun or pronoun and a participle (*the sun having risen*), is another kind of sentence modifier. Absolute phrases are not connected to the remainder of the sentence by relating words such as prepositions or conjunctions. They are therefore set off by commas.

The river being cold, we did not go swimming.

It seemed sensible, *the weather being warm,* to pack a lunch .

To Set Off a Long Phrase or Clause Preceding the Subject

Since the first element in an English sentence is normally its subject, any phrase or clause of five words or more preceding the subject is concluded with a comma to indicate that the subject is about to appear.

During the long winter of 1881, the king suffered a severe illness.

When I see robins on the lawn, I know that spring is here.

Having reached the age of discretion, she was no longer supervised.

If the phrase is so short that the reader can take in both the phrase and the subject in a single glance, the comma is not necessary.

In 1881 the king suffered a severe illness.

To Indicate Interruptions of Normal Word Order

Set off by commas any words, phrases, or clauses that interrupt normal word order. Normally, adjectives precede the nouns they modify, and, normally, subjects are followed by verbs or by modifying phrases or clauses:

> The old and respected firm went bankrupt.

If, for purpose of emphasis, the adjectives *old* and *respected* follow the noun *firm,* they are set off by commas:

> The firm, old and respected, went bankrupt.

A single comma should never interrupt the natural flow of a sentence, as from subject to verb or from verb to verb completion. But intruding elements of any kind should be preceded and followed by commas.

> The river, it seems likely, will overflow its banks.

> The year of his graduation, 1950, was an eventful one.

> She was a tall and, to put it mildly, buxom woman

To Set Off Nonrestrictive Elements

Any word, phrase, or clause that is not essential to the meaning of a sentence is called nonrestrictive. Set off nonrestrictive elements by commas.

> Some words, like *scurrilous,* are difficult to spell.

> His father, Mr. Smith, was ill.

> The Homeric epics, the *Iliad* and the *Odyssey,* are long poems.

His uncle, who is a doctor, is coming for a visit.

Be careful to distinguish between such nonrestrictive elements and restrictive elements. Restrictive words, phrases, or clauses are necessary to the meaning of a sentence and are never set off by commas.

Shakespeare's play *Hamlet* is a masterpiece.
(The name of the play is essential to the meaning.)

Dante's epic, *The Divine Comedy,* is made up of one hundred cantos.
(It is Dante's only epic; its name is therefore not essential.)

The people who sat in the balcony paid less for their seats.
(The clause *who sat in the balcony* is restrictive.)

My brother, who sat in the balcony, enjoyed the play.
(The location of his seat is not considered essential to the statement being made.)

By insertion or omission of commas, the writer can indicate whether elements are restrictive or not.

His dog Rover is a collie.
(The lack of commas indicates that he has several dogs. One of them is named Rover.)

His dog, Rover, is a collie.
(He owns only one dog. The name is given but it is not essential.)

When the nonrestrictive element occurs at the end of the sentence, the comma preceding it indicates its relative unimportance.

The president was interviewed by a large group of reporters, who were informally dressed.

To Separate Contrasted Sentence Elements

Use the comma to emphasize the contrast between two parts of a sentence.

> He wanted to see a psychiatrist, not a lawyer.

> His diet was wholesome, not appetizing.

> She longed to find happiness, but found misery instead.

To Prevent Misreading

Use the comma to prevent misreading when the sequence of words in a sentence might lead to momentary confusion.

> During the summer, days become longer.

Without the comma, the reader might well read *summer days* as adjectival-noun.

> Soon after, the meeting was adjourned.

Without the comma, the reader might read *after the meeting* as a prepositional phrase, and this fragment would have no subject.

> The lawyer interviewed John and Fred, and seemed very happy about what they had to say.

In this sentence the two *and*'s occur in close proximity. The first joins the nouns *John* and *Fred;* the second joins the verbs *interviewed* and *seemed.* The comma after *Fred* clarifies the structure of the sentence.

Conventional Uses of the Comma

Certain uses of the comma have become established by convention.

➤ Following the salutation of an informal letter: *Dear Mildred,*

➤ Following the complimentary close of a letter: *Yours truly,*

➤ Separating dates of the month from the year: *June 19, 1942*

➤ Separating parts of an address: *Mr. John Smith, 138 Elm Street, Syracuse, N.Y. 13082*

➤ Separating numbered or lettered divisions or subdivisions: *Book III, Chapter 9;* or *III, 9;* or *A, d*

➤ Separating names from distinguishing titles: *Frank Jones, Jr.* or *Edward French, Ph.D.*

➤ Separating thousands in large figures: *1,497,341*

➤ Separating a direct quotation from the indication of the speaker.

➤ Placed before and after introductory words and abbreviations such as *i.e., e.g.,* and *for example: Some plays are known as closet dramas; i.e., they were written to be read rather than acted.*

MISUSE OF THE COMMA

Do not annoy the reader by inserting commas where they are not required. Commas are intended to help the reader; unnecessary commas only confuse.

Do Not Interrupt the Normal Flow of Thought by a Comma

WRONG: The fact that the train had broken down halfway between its point of departure

and its destination, was sufficient reason
for the passengers to malign the railroad.
(Never separate the subject from the predicate
with a comma. The subject is a long clause,
but it is entirely clear. It opens the sentence as
expected, and it is followed immediately by
the verb. Inserting a comma after *destination*
merely impedes the flow of thought.)

WRONG: The carpenter insisted, that he knew what
he was doing.
(The comma after *insisted* separates the verb
from its object.)

WRONG: He drove a hard, sharp, painful, bargain.
(The comma after *painful* separates the adjective *painful* from the word it modifies.)

Do Not Separate Words or Phrases Joined by *And* or *Or*

WRONG: He went to the office, and opened his
mail.
(*And* joins the compound verb *went* and
opened. It does not join two clauses.)

Do Not Place a Comma Between a Conjunction and the Word or Words It Introduces

WRONG: He was tired but, he refused to stop driving.

WRONG: The lonely woman continued to hope that, her
son was still alive.

THE SEMICOLON

The semicolon functions midway between the comma and the period as an indication of a pause. It is stronger than the comma and weaker than the period.

To Separate Independent Clauses

The principal use of the semicolon is to mark the dividing point in a compound sentence, the clauses of which are not joined by a coordinating conjunction.

> The policeman stood on the corner; he was watching the traffic pattern at the intersection.

> The boss had a good sense of humor; nevertheless, he was a strict supervisor.

To Separate Major Word Groupings from Lesser Ones

A proliferation of commas in a sentence may lead to confusion. The semicolon, as a stronger mark, is therefore useful in punctuating major elements that themselves contain commas.

> He visited several colleges, schools, and institutions; several factories, office buildings, and churches; and a number of public buildings of a miscellaneous nature.
> (The three major divisions, the first two of which contain commas, are clarified by the use of the semicolon.)

> The old horse, tired and hungry after its long journey over the long, hilly, rutted country roads, finally

staggered and fell; and it was a long time before it could be persuaded to get up again.

(The individual clauses of the compound sentence, the first of which contains several commas, are clearly indicated by the semicolon.)

THE COLON

The colon means *as follows*. It is principally used to introduce a list (frequently in conjunction with such words as *following* or *as follows*). It should not be used to introduce a short list such as **He grew: beans, peas, and apples.*

Five merchants contributed to the fund: John Doe, Frank Smith, Eliot Doolittle, Ezra Jones, and Samuel Greenbaum.

The principles on which the club was founded are as follows:

1. The establishment of a revolving fund for education.

2. The provision of entertainment for the children.

3. Monthly social meetings for the adults.

Occasionally the colon is used to introduce a single word or phrase to add dramatic significance.

He had only one thing to live for: death.

The colon can be used to introduce a single word, phrase, or clause when it acts as a substitute for the words *as a result*.

The president died: the firm failed.

The colon is used after the salutation of a business letter (*Dear Sir:* or *To Whom It May Concern:*) and to divide subdivisions from major divisions, as in recording time (*12:25*) or Biblical references (*Genesis 10:3*).

THE DASH

The dash is used to indicate a sharp or sudden break in the normal or expected flow of sentence structure. (In typing, a dash is represented by two hyphens.)

> He asked me—what was he thinking?—to marry him.

> I hoped that he—. But I'd rather not talk about it.

The dash may be used to separate parenthetical ideas or ideas inserted as an afterthought.

PARENTHETICAL: The New York skyline—especially when viewed for the first time—is a breathtaking sight.

AFTERTHOUGHT: He ran down the hill with the speed of an express train—or so it seemed.

The dash is used in dialogue to describe hesitating or halting speech.

> "I mean—I think—I think I mean," he began hesitantly. "I think I mean I'd make a good husband."

THE HYPHEN

The hyphen is used to make a compound word out of two or more words that are intended to be read as a single unit.

The Dartmouth-Brown game

Mr. John King-Smith

A high-pressure salesman

A red-faced culprit

A holier-than-thou expression

The hyphen is used to eliminate ambiguities or mis-readings which occasionally result from the addition of a prefix.

re-press   re-call   re-sign

The hyphen is used to indicate that the remainder of a word is to follow when the word is broken at the end of a line. Words may not be divided arbitrarily; they may be broken only between syllables. (Syllables are the parts of a word which are naturally pronounced as units. When in doubt about correct division into syllables, consult a good dictionary.)

Samuel Johnson, who was an outstanding literary figure of the eighteenth century in England, was known as the great lexicographer. He compiled the first English dictionary.

The hyphen is used with compound numbers from *twenty-one* to *ninety-nine.*

The hyphen is used to separate dates of birth and death: *John Barton* (1181-1214); scores of games: 13-12; and other figures where the relationship between them is obvious.

THE APOSTROPHE

Apart from indicating possession, the apostrophe is principally used to indicate letters in a contraction.

Who's there? I can't come.

The apostrophe is also used to form plurals of letters, figures, or signs for which there is no acceptable plural.

There are three 9's, twenty-seven *n*'s, and two *'s on the page.

PARENTHESES AND BRACKETS

Parentheses are used to enclose materials that are so intrusive as to be an annoying interruption of sentence structure.

It is important (importance being understood to be a relative matter) to obey the law.

The law was passed (1) to satisfy the governor, (2) to please the people, and (3) to provide greater safety.

The houses were classified as (*a*) bungalows, (*b*) ranch-type houses, (*c*) split-level houses.

His novel *The Homeward Trail* (1917) was a best-seller.

Brackets are used to enclose additions by the editor to any kind of quoted matter.

"The author [Mark Twain] was known primarily as a humorist."

"He was born in 1835 [?] in a small southern town."

QUOTATIONS AND QUOTATION MARKS

Quotation Marks to Indicate Titles

Quotations marks are used to indicate titles of short works such as articles in magazines, short stories, one-act plays, essays, short poems, and chapter titles.

"The Raven"   (short poem)

"The Murders in the Rue Morgue"   (short story)

"Bound East for Cardiff"   (one-act play)

Direct Quotations

Quoted materials, whether oral or written, are indicated by being enclosed in quotation marks. Only the exact words of the original speaker or writer should be so enclosed. An indirect quotation or a report of the substance of what was said or written should not be enclosed by quotation marks.

DIRECT:	He said, "I am going home."
INDIRECT:	He said that he was going home.
DIRECT:	She said, "I have a headache. I am going to bed."
INDIRECT:	She said that her head hurt and that she was going to bed.
DIRECT:	The opening words of the chapter are "I continued at home with my wife and children."

INDIRECT: The opening words of the chapter state that the author stayed at home with his wife and children.

COMBINED: She said that she had "no intentions" of staying.

In direct quotations, indications of the speaker (*he said, she asked*) are separated from the quotation by a comma or marked off by two commas if reference to the speaker is placed within a sentence.

> "Please don't tell my mother," he whined.

> The nurse replied, "That's exactly what I intend to do."

> "Well, at least," he entreated, "don't tell her everything."

When the indication of the speaker is placed at the end of a quotation that concludes with a question mark or an exclamation mark, the comma is omitted.

> "Don't you know enough to stop?" he asked.

> "Let me go!" she shrieked.

If the quotation consists of more than one sentence, only one sentence is joined to the indication of the speaker.

> "My son wants to buy this," she said. "How much will it cost?"

> "I wouldn't do that," he remonstrated. "You might get into trouble."

In quotations other than dialogue, the punctuation and capitalization of quoted matter is reproduced exactly as it was originally written.

The author believes that "Capitalism is here to stay."

The novel reflected the author's "growing concern with the problem of juvenile delinquency."

If the quotation is longer than one paragraph, no end quotation marks are placed at the conclusion of the first paragraph. All succeeding paragraphs are prefaced by quotation marks, but only the final paragraph is concluded with end quotation marks.

Long quotations (ten lines or more) from writings are not enclosed in quotation marks. They are set off from the original writing by indentation. Smaller typeface is customary for printed matter and single spacing for typewritten material.

Quotations Within Quotations

Single quotation marks are used to indicate a quotation within a quotation.

"I've just read Shelley's 'Ode to the West Wind,'" she said.

The alternation of double and single quotation marks is continued for the inclusion of quotations within quotations within other quotations. Such complexities should be avoided, of course, but the following is an example of the technique:

"Are you aware," asked the lawyer, "that the defendant precisely stated, 'I did not read "The Bride Said, 'No'"'?"

Be sure that all opening quotation marks are balanced by end quotation marks.

Quotation Marks Used with Other Punctuation

The placing of quotation marks in connection with other punctuation follows the standard procedures instituted by printers for the sake of the physical appearance of the page. Periods and commas are always placed inside end quotation marks.

> "I wanted," he said, "to go home."

Colons and semicolons are always placed outside end quotation marks. Other marks are placed where they logically belong—within the quotation if they punctuate the quotation, outside the quotation if they punctuate the sentence of which the quotation is a part.

> He called his friend "old frog"; he didn't mean it as an insult.

> He assimilated the advice given in the pamphlet "How to Study"; he passed the course.

> "How are you?" I asked.

> How can I tell that "Whatever is, is right"?

> Beware of "the valley of the shadow of death"!

Punctuation of Dialogue

Standard practice in the punctuation of dialogue calls for a new paragraph for each change of speaker. Descriptive or other materials related to the speaker are contained in the same paragraph as the quotation.

> "I knew it!" said the toper to the shepherd with much satisfaction. "When I walked up your garden before coming in, and saw the hives all of a row, I

said to myself, 'Where there's bees, there's honey, and where there's honey, there's mead.' But mead of such a truly comfortable sort as this I really didn't expect to meet in my older days." He took yet another pull at the mug, till it assumed an ominous elevation.

"Glad you enjoy it!" said the shepherd, warmly.

"It is a goodish mead," assented Mrs. Fennel, with an absence of enthusiasm which seemed to say that it was possible to buy praise for one's cellar at too heavy a price. "It is trouble enough to make, and really I hardly think we shall make any more. For honey sells well, and we ourselves can make shift with a drop o' small mead and metheglin for common use from the comb-washings."

"Oh, but you'll never have the heart!" reproachfully cried the stranger in cinder-gray, after taking up the mug a third time and setting it down empty.

"I love mead when 'tis old like this, as I love to go to church o' Sundays, or to relieve the needy any day of the week."

"Ha, ha, ha!" said the man in the chimney-corner, who, in spite of the taciturnity induced by the pipe of tobacco, could not or would not refrain from this slight testimony to his comrade's humor.

— Thomas Hardy, "The Three Strangers"

A particular advantage of this convention is that when only two speakers are involved, the alternation of paragraphs makes it unnecessary to identify each speaker in turn and allows the dialogue to be paced more rapidly and without interruptions.

"Everybody believed the story, didn't they?" said the dirty-faced man, refilling his pipe.

"Except Tom's enemies," replied the bagman. "Some of 'em said Tom invented it altogether; and others said he was drunk, and fancied it, and got hold of the wrong trousers by mistake before he went to bed. But nobody ever minded what they said."

"Tom said it was all true?"

"Every word."

"And your uncle?"

"Every letter."

"They must have been very nice men, both of 'em," said the dirty-faced man.

"Yes, they were," replied the bagman; "very nice men indeed!"

— Charles Dickens, "The Bagman's Story"

ITALICS

Italics is a term used to designate a particular font of printer's type in which the letters slant upwards to the right as in the word *italics*. In written or typed material, italics are indicated by underlining.

Italics to Indicate Titles of Full-Length Works

Use italics to indicate the titles of novels, full-length plays, long book-length poems, full-length motion pictures, and the titles of books in general. They are also used to indicate names of magazines or periodical publications of any sort. This usage in conjunction with quotation marks helps to distinguish the chapter from the complete book, the poem from the collection in which it appears, the article from the magazine, etc.

Hamlet   A Tale of Two Cities   The Atlantic Monthly

EXCEPTIONS: Through convention, the Bible and the books of the Bible are neither italicized nor put in quotation marks. The place of publication of newspapers (normally regarded as part of the title) is frequently not italicized.

Genesis   *The New York Times*   The Iowa *Gazette*

Italics to Indicate Words or Letters Used as Such

Use italics to indicate words or letters which are used as such, that is, words or letters considered independent of their meaning.

The word *benign* is sometimes misspelled.

The letter *I* should be capitalized when used alone.

Italics for Emphasis

Italics are occasionally used (though very rarely) to give emphasis to a particular word or group of words. This usage should be avoided and resorted to only when no other method of stressing the word is available, as in the reporting of dialogue or in the writing of plays.

"I didn't mean your husband; I meant *you!*"

Chapter 7
Wordiness

Although it is not concerned with grammar, a common fault in writing is the use of excessive words to convey intended meaning. A writing style that will command the reader's attention must be concise and free of the "deadwood" that clutters sentences.

AVOIDING WORDINESS

Cut Out Useless Introductory Phrases

Some writers acquire the insidious (and boring) habit of beginning sentences with long and useless introductory phrases or clauses. In the following examples, all sentences would be improved by eliminating italicized words.

> *With reference to your question,* I think we should go on Thursday.

> *It goes without saying that* the poor who are helpless need assistance.

> *At that point in time,* he had no vocational goal.

> *By way of response,* I will second the motion.

> *It seems unnecessary to point out that* it is now raining.

Cut Out Deadwood Within the Body of a Sentence

Two of the chief enemies of student writers who attempt to achieve economical writing styles are *redundancy* and *circumlocution*. Although the end result in both cases is wordiness, there are distinct differences between the two terms.

➤ *Redundancy is* the term for using words that needlessly repeat the meaning. For example, there is no need to say "advance planning"; planning is always done in advance. Other redundant phrases that should be avoided are *close* proximity, *end* result, *grateful* thanks, *habitual* custom, *local* resident, *mutual* cooperation, *old* adage, *past* history, *self*-confessed, *successful* achievements, *true* facts, *usual* customs, and *young* teenager.

➤ *Circumlocution* means literally "talking around" a subject. The following examples of this type of wordiness should be replaced by the words in parentheses that follow:

> *ahead of schedule* (early)
> *am in possession* (have)
> *at an early date* (soon)
> *at this point in time* (now)
> *best of health* (well)
> *caused injuries to* (injured)
> *draw attention to* (point out)
> *during the time that* (while)
> *give rise to* (cause)
> *in advance of* (before)
> *in the event that* (if)
> *in this day and age* (today)
> *made a statement saying* (stated or *said*)

> *made an escape* (escaped)
> *owing to the fact that* (because)
> *put in an appearance* (appeared)
> *render assistance to* (help)
> *succumbed to injuries* (died)
> *take action on the issue* (acted)
> *the reason why is that* (because)
> *this is a topic that* (this topic)
> *was of the opinion that* (thought)
> *was witness to* (saw)

Avoid the Constructions *It Is* . . . and *There are* . . .

Almost every time sentences begin with *It is* or *There are* wordiness results, as the following examples demonstrate:

> It is time which heals all wounds.
> Time heals all wounds.
>
> There are some writers who cannot help being wordy.
> Some writers cannot help being wordy.
>
> It is to be expected that politicians are wordy.
> Politicians are expected to be wordy.
>
> There are many persons who find writing difficult.
> Many persons find writing difficult.

Chapter 8

Glossary of Words and Phrases Frequently Misused

a, an   Use *a* before words beginning with a consonant sound: *a book, a unique necklace.* Use *an* before words beginning with a vowel sound: *an apple, an urchin.* NOTE: It is the sound, not the actual letter, that determines the form of the indefinite article: *a university, an R.C.A. television set, an eight-sided object.*

accept, except   *Accept* means to receive: "Please *accept* my offer." The verb *except* means to leave out: "Will you *except* the last provision of the contract?"

adapt, adopt   *Adapt* incorporates the word *apt,* which means *suited to the purpose;* therefore, *adapt* means *to make suitable. Adopt* means *to choose* or *to make one's own selection.* "We *adopted* the style of play that had been *adapted* from the style used by the Green Bay Packers."

adverse, averse   *Adverse* means *opposing: adverse circumstances. Averse* means *disinclined:* "He was *averse* to my proposal." *Adverse is* usually related to actions or things, *averse* to people (who have an aversion).

advert, avert   *Advert* means *refer:* "The speaker *adverted* to an earlier talk he had given." *Avert* means *ward off:* "He narrowly *averted* a bad fall."

affect, effect *Affect* means to *influence:* "His attitude in class *affected* his grade." *Affect* is never used as a noun except in psychological terminology, where it refers to a feeling or emotion, rather than thought or action, *Effect* as a noun means *result:* "The *effect* of the explosion was disastrous." *Effect* as a verb means to *accomplish:* "The new machinery *effected* a decided improvement in the product."

aggravate Do not use *aggravate* to mean *irritate.* *Aggravate* means to make a bad situation worse.

aid, aide *Aid,* meaning to assist, can be a verb: "Alice will *aid* the toddlers in tying their shoes." *Aid* can also be a noun: "Robert gave *aid* to the homeless." *Aide* is always a noun meaning an assistant: "The general had an excellent *aide* to assist him."

ain't A word used in writing only in dialogue or in an attempt to be humorous.

all ready, already *All ready,* an adjective, means everyone is in readiness or properly prepared: "We were *all ready* to go." *Already,* an adverb, means previously: "They had *already* gone.".

allusion, illusion, delusion An *allusion* is an indirect reference to a literary work or to a statement by another: "When she said, 'To go or not to go, that is the question,' Betty was using an *allusion* to *Hamlet.*" An *illusion* is something that appears real to the perception, but is not: "Richard realized that although the magician seemed to be sawing a woman in half, it was an *illusion.*" A *delusion* is also a false perception about one's self or others, but is based more on a set of false beliefs than an unreal image: "Although he had achieved very little in school, Joseph had *delusions* of grandeur."

alot An incorrect spelling of the much overused phrase *a lot.*

alright A bad spelling of *all right.* Do not confuse the spelling with words like *almost, already, altogether.*

alumnus, alumna, alumni, alumnae An *alumnus* is a male graduate. *Alumni* is the plural. An *alumna* is a female graduate. *Alumnae* is the plural. *Alumni* is used for male and female combined.

alternate, alternative *Alternate* as a verb means to function every other time or to act by turns: "Travis and Jason will *alternate* playing the Nintendo game." *Alternate* as a noun means one who takes the place of another: "On the debating team, Lindsey served as an *alternate.*" *Alternative,* also a noun, refers to a choice between two possibilities, one of which must be rejected: "Her only *alternative* was to leave immediately or remain longer than she wished."

a.m., p.m. (or A.M., P.M.) Use only with numbers. *The matinee began at 3:00 p.m.* (never *at three in the p.m.*)

ambivalent, ambiguous *Ambivalent* means mixed or conflicting feelings about a person or an idea. *Ambiguous* is a statement capable of being misinterpreted because it is not clear.

amend, emend *Amend* means to alter for the better, as in *amendments* to the Constitution. *Emend,* once an alternative spelling for *amend,* now is specialized in use to mean removing errors from a text.

amiable, amicable *Amiable* is used to describe persons who are kind, gentle, and friendly. *Amicable* is used to describe arrangements or settlements which are agreed to peacefully by both parties.

among, between *Between* is used in connection with two persons or things. "He divided the money *between* his two sons." *Among* is used for more than two: "He divided the money *among* his three sons." EXCEPTIONS: If more than two are involved in a united situation, *between* is used: "*Between* the four of us we raised a thousand dollars." If a comparison or an opposition is involved, *between* is used: "There was great rivalry *between* the three colleges. It was difficult to choose *between* them."

amount, number   *Amount* refers to bulk or quantity: *amount* of sugar, grain, flour, money. *Number* refers to objects which are thought of as individual units; *number* of oranges, children, diamonds. Notice that most words following *amount* are singular (*coal, butter, water*) and that most words following *number* are plural (*apples, bottles, cups*).

and etc.   This is repetitious, and the *and* should be omitted. *Etc.* is an abbreviation of the Latin *et cetera*, meaning *and other things.*

and/or   Although the legalism *and/or* is becoming common in current English, it is to be avoided as faddish verbiage. The simple word *or* carries exactly the same meaning in most cases and does not call attention to itself.

ante-, anti-   These prefixes, though similar, are quite different in meaning. *Ante-* means *before,* as in *antechamber* (a small room that comes before a larger one) or *antebellum* (before the war). *Anti-* means opposed to, as in *antinuclear* or *antitoxin.*

anyways, anywheres   Incorrect spellings of *anyway* and *anywhere.*

appraise, apprise   *Appraise* means to evaluate; apprise means to inform: "The jeweler *appraised* the diamond and *apprised* the owner of his evaluation."

apprehend, comprehend   *Comprehend* means only to understand a communication; *apprehend* carries that meaning as well as anticipating with dread or anxiety, with the adjective form used more often: "Sarah was *apprehensive* about flying." *Comprehensive* means all-inclusive, or covering completely: "The insurance policy was *comprehensive*."

apt, liable, likely   *Apt* refers to a habitual disposition: "Having a good brain, he is apt to get high grades." *Likely* merely expresses probability: "It is *likely* to rain." *Liable* implies the probability of something unfortunate: "The firm is *liable* to fail."

as, like   When used as a preposition, *like* should never introduce a clause (NOT *like I was saying*). When introducing a clause, *as* is used *(as I was saying)* even if some of the words of the clause are implied: "He did it as well *as* I [did]."

ascent, assent   *Ascent* is a noun referring to a climb or movement upward; *assent* is a noun or verb having to do with agreement with an idea or an opinion: "Eugenia *assented* (or gave *assent*) to the group's opinion that the weather was too uncertain for an *ascent* up the mountain."

awful   Never use this adjective in such sentences as "she is *awful* nice."

beside, besides   *Beside* means *by the side of*: "Ask him to sit *beside* me." *Besides* means in addition: "She had an apartment in the city. *Besides*, she owned a home at the shore."

bimonthly, semimonthly   *Bimonthly* means occurring every two months; *semimonthly* means twice a month. This can be applied to *biweekly, semiweekly* and *biennial, semiannual*.

bring, take *Bring* refers to action toward the writer or speaker: "*Bring* the book to me." *Take* refers to action away from the writer or speaker: "When you leave us, *take* your books with you."

burst, bust *Burst*, meaning to explode or erupt from inward pressure, is sometimes written *bust*, but this is slang and is incorrect.

can, may *Can* implies ability: "I *can* (I am able to) swim." *May* denotes permission: "*May* I (Have I permission to) swim in your pool?" In informal speech, when the context is clear, *can* and *may* are both used to express permission.

can't hardly, can't scarcely Avoid these double negatives by using *can hardly* and *can scarcely*.

capital, capitol *Capital* denotes the seat of government of a state or nation. *Capitol* is the building in which a legislative assembly meets.

censure, criticize, censor To *censure* always expresses disapproval, but to *criticize* may be neutral, expressing approval of some characteristics and disapproval of others. *Criticism* should be a careful weighing of the merits and demerits of such things as artistic works. *Censor* means to "suppress what are considered to be objectionable words or ideas."

cite, site To *cite* is to make a reference to an original source when you are writing a research essay. The noun *site* applies to the space of ground occupied or to be occupied by a building: "The *site* of a new bank."

claim, assert *Claim* refers to a justified demand or legal right: "I *claim* this piece of property." "I *claim* the prize." It should not be used when only an assertion is involved; "He *asserted* (not *claimed*) that his demands were reasonable."

compare to, compare with *Compare to* is used to indicate a definite resemblance: "He compared the railroad *to* a street." *Compare with* is used to indicate an examination of similarities and dissimilarities: "He compared the Middle Ages *with* modern times."

complement, compliment A *complement* is something that fills up or completes, as in the sentence: "Foreign travel is a *complement* to the study of geography." A *compliment* is, of course, an expression of praise, as in "He paid her a high *compliment.*"

comprehensible, comprehensive *Comprehensible* means capable of being understood. *Comprehensive* means all-inclusive or covering a wide range of knowledge on a subject.

compulsion, compunction *Compulsion* is to be compelled to action by a psychological urge. *Compunction* is to feel anxiety because of guilt or remorse.

confidant, confident A *confidant* (*confidante,* if female) is a noun meaning a trusted friend. *Confident* is an adjective meaning you are certain, e.g., you are *confident* he or she will not betray your trust.

congenital, congenial A *congenital* defect is a bodily defect dating from birth. A *congenial* person is pleasant and sociable.

connotation, denotation The *connotation* of a word is what it suggests, favorably or unfavorably, beyond its dictionary meaning (*denotation*). For example, *steed denotes horse,* but *connotes* a powerful, beautiful horse ridden by a knight, unlike *nag,* which suggests a broken-down horse.

consensus   Even in respected newspapers, *consensus* is sometimes misspelled "consensus," perhaps in the mistaken idea that a "census" has been taken to determine agreement. The root word has to do with consent, hence *consensus*. Do not use the phrase *consensus of opinion*, which is redundant.

contemptible, contemptuous   *Contemptible* is something that deserves contempt. A *contemptuous* person shows disdain for a person or thing.

continual, continuous   A *continual* action occurs over a considerable period of time with pauses and intermissions: "He censured her *continually*. " A *continuous* action occurs without such pauses: "The roar of the waterfall was *continuous*."

cool   Virtually meaningless and much overused as an adjective complimenting an action. Use precise words that show why you like it.

counselor, counselor   A *councilor* is a member of a council. A *counselor* advises, particularly on legal matters.

counsel, council   *Counsel* as a noun means advice, or, in legal parlance, a lawyer or lawyers: "He sought my *counsel*." "He retained *counsel* to represent him at the trial." As a verb *counsel* means to *advise*: "I would *counsel* you to accept the first good offer." *Council* is a group of individuals who act in advisory capacity or who meet for the purposes of discussion or decision making: "The mayor met with the *council*." "They called a *council* to make plans for the future."

credible, credulous   *Credible* means believable (or capable of being believed) and is the opposite of *incredible*. A *credulous* person is willing to believe even when the evidence is not conclusive.

deadly, deathly   A poison is *deadly* if it can cause death. Silence is *deathly* if it is like the silence of death but does not kill.

deduce, deduct   To *deduce* means using reasoning to derive a conclusion. To *deduct*, you subtract, for example, a discount of 10 percent from a price.

deprecate, depredate   To *deprecate* is to express disapproval. To *depreciate* is to lessen the value of an item.

detract, distract   Although both of these words mean to draw away from, *detract* has come to mean taking away someone's good name, as in "His constant lying *detracts* from his good qualities." *Distract* means drawing the mind away from whatever it had been thinking, as in "The loud noise *distracted* her making her lose concentration."

different from   *Different from* is the correct idiom, NOT *different than.*

differ from, differ with   *Differ from* applies to differences between one person or thing and others: "My car *differs from* his because it is a newer model." *Differ with* means to have a difference in opinion: "I *differ with* him in his views about government. "

discover, invent   You *discover* something already in existence, but unknown (like electricity); you *invent* a new product, like a video recorder.

discreet, discrete   *Discreet* means careful in avoiding mistakes, as in "He was *discreet* in his habits." *Discrete* means separate, or detached, as in "Each grain of rice was *discrete,* not clinging to the rest in a glutinous mass."

disinterested, uninterested   *Disinterested* means impartial, showing no preference or prejudice. To be *uninterested is* to be bored, or simply lacking interest.

don't   *Don't* is the contraction of *do not: I don't, you don't, we don't, they don't.* Do not confuse it with *doesn't,* the contraction of *does not: He doesn't, she doesn't, it doesn't.*

dual, duel   *Dual* always refers to two things, as in a "dual-control" video game. *Duel* refers to a formal contest with guns or pistols.

due to   *Due to* functions like the adjective *attributable* plus the preposition *to.* "The *flood* was *attributable to* the rapid spring thaw." "The *flood* was *due to* the rapid spring thaw." If there is no noun like *flood* for the adjective *due to* to refer to, use the preposition *because of*: "He was late *because of* an accident." Or rephrase the sentence: "His *lateness* was *due to* an accident."

elicit, illicit   *Elicit,* always a verb, means to draw forth or bring out: "Herman can always *elicit* an argument with anyone." *Illicit,* always an adjective, means unlawful: "*Illicit* drugs cause major problems in this country."

eminent, imminent   *Eminent* means famous or prominent; *imminent* means soon to take place: "The Christmas season is *imminent.*"

enormity, enormousness   *Enormity,* used to describe something monstrously evil, should never be confused with *enormousness,* which refers to something of extraordinarily large size.

enthused   *Enthusiastic* is correct in formal writing, not *enthused*. "She was *enthusiastic* about her class in creative writing."

farther, further   *Farther* refers to physical distance: "We will drive no *farther* tonight." *Further* refers to degree or extent: "Let's pursue this argument no *further.*"

fewer, less   *Fewer* is used in connection with people or with objects that are thought of as individual units: *fewer oranges, fewer children,* fewer *books, fewer dollars* . *Less* is used in connection with the concept of bulk: *less money, less coal, less weight, less grain.* Notice that most words following *fewer* are plural (*oranges, books, dollars*); most words following *less* are singular (*money, coal, wheat*).

flotsam, jetsam   *Flotsam* means wreckage found afloat. *Jetsam,* which comes from the word *jettison,* means objects thrown overboard and then washed ashore.

forceful, forcible   One can have *a forceful* personality, but to break down a door violently is to make a *forcible* entry.

former, latter   *Former* and *latter* are used to designate one of *two* persons or things: "Of the *two* possibilities, I prefer the *former* to the *latter.*" If more than two persons or things are involved, *first* or *first named* and *last* or *last named* are used: "He had a choice of yellow, rose, pink, and brown. He preferred the *first* and *last* to the others."

fortuitous, fortunate   That which is *fortuitous* happens by accident and may or may not be a favorable event. The word is often misused as a synonym for *fortunate,* but it does not have this meaning.

founder, flounder   *Founder,* a nautical verb, denotes
a boat collapsing or sinking. Anyone can *flounder,*
which means to move clumsily about or to struggle
to gain footing: "He *floundered* in the deep mud."

fulsome   Never use *fulsome* to mean plentiful; it
means excessive and insincere: "Her boss gave
fulsome praise, which angered her."

had ought   *Ought* is known as a defective verb
because it has only one form and cannot be used
with an auxiliary: "They *ought* (NOT *had ought*) to
have told her."

hanged, hung   *Hanged* is used in connection with
executions: "He was condemned to be *hanged* by
the neck until dead." *Hung* denotes any other kind
of suspension: "The pictures were *hung* on the
wall."

hardly   Like *barely* and *scarcely, hardly* should not
be used with a negative. "He was *hardly* (*barely,
scarcely*) able to do it." (NOT *not hardly, barely,
scarcely*)

healthful, healthy   *Healthful* means *health-giving:* a
healthful climate. *Healthy* means *in a state of
health:* "He was a *healthy* young man."

hypercritical, hypocritical   A *hypercritical* person is
overly critical; a *hypocritical* individual does not
practice what he or she advises.

imply, infer   *Imply* means to throw out a hint or
suggestion: "She *implied* by her manner that she
was unhappy." *Infer* means to take in a hint or
suggestion: "I *inferred* from her manner that she
was unhappy."

impracticable, impractical   *Impracticable* means
impossible to put into practice. *Impractical,* when

referring to a person, means one who is incapable of dealing sensibly with practical (or day-to-day) matters. A plan may be *impractical* if it is not profit-making.

intense, intensive   *Intense* means something is present to a high or extreme degree, for example, *intense* suffering. *Intensive* means highly concentrated or exhaustive in application, as in the Intensive Care Unit of a hospital.

invaluable, priceless   Usually, the prefix *in-* indicates a negative, but *invaluable* does not mean "of no value." It means that the value of the object is so great that its worth cannot be evaluated. The word *priceless* has the same meaning: " so great a value that a price cannot be set for it."

its, it's   *Its* (no apostrophe) is the possessive case of *it*: "The pig nursed *its* young." *It's* is the contraction for *it is*: "*It's* too late to do anything about it."

kind, sort, type, variety   Since these words are singular in number, they should never be prefaced by plural demonstrative pronouns: *This kind of people* (NOT *these kind of people*).

kind of, sort of, type of, variety of   Never use *a* or *an* after these expressions. *Kind of a pistol is confusing because *a* is used for one particular member of a class; whereas *kind of pistol* is preferable because *pistol* by itself correctly refers to the general idea of *pistol*.

lack, absence   *Lack* is a deficiency of something needed: "The *lack* of rain ruined the crops." *Absence* is the nonpresence of a thing that may or may not be necessary: "The *absence* of malice in the negotiations between the parties allowed them to move faster."

last, latest   *Last* means that which comes at the end: "It is the *last* game of the season." *Latest* is the last in time, but not necessarily the final occurrence: "That was the *latest* insult in a series of indignities."

lay, lie   *Lay, laid, laid* are the principal parts of the transitive verb which means *to put down:* "I shall *lay* the rug." "I *laid* the rug." "I have *laid* the rug." *Lie, lay, lain* are the principal parts of the intransitive verb (it cannot take an object) which means *to recline* or *repose:* "She will *lie* in the hammock." "She *is lying* in the hammock." "She *lay* in the hammock yesterday." "She *has lain* there all afternoon."

lead, led   When pronounced alike the noun *lead* is the metal, *led* is the past tense and past participle of the verb *to lead.*

learn, teach   *Learn* means to acquire information or knowledge: "I *learned* my lesson." *Teach* means to impart information or knowledge: "I *taught* him to do it."

liable   See *apt.*

like   See *as.*

literally, figuratively   Unless an event actually happened (*literally* happened), one speaks of it *figuratively.* One should not say, "We *literally* died laughing." *Figuratively* refers to the use of figures of speech, such as similes or metaphors: "When he forgot his wife's birthday, he was in (NOT *literally*) the doghouse."

lose, loose   *Lose* is a verb: "Did you *lose* your credit card?" *Loose* is an adjective: "Your belt is *loose.*"

lots   Informal word meaning *many, much.*

mean, median *Mean* is the middle point between extremes, usually the arithmetic *mean* (computed by dividing the sum of quantities in a set by the number of terms in the set). *Median* refers to the middle value in a distribution: "The *median* salary in the organization is larger than half and smaller than half of all the salaries."

meantime, meanwhile The noun *meantime* refers to an action taking place in an interim: "In the *meantime,* he read the novel." The adverb *meanwhile is* almost the same in meaning: "*Meanwhile,* he read the novel."

militate, mitigate *Militate* (connected with militate) means to have strong influence for or against, usually against: "His grouchy manner *militated* against his success as a salesman." *Mitigate* means to *lessen:* "The cold compress on his leg *mitigated* his suffering."

myself *Myself* (like *yourself, himself, herself, itself, themselves*) is an intensive and reflexive pronoun. It should never be used in a sentence without its corresponding noun or pronoun: "I *myself* will do it." "I hurt *myself.*" "They sent for John and *me* (NOT *myself*)."

mysterious, mystic *Mysterious* refers to those phenomena that excite wonder, curiosity, and surprise and that are difficult to explain or understand. A *mystic* purports to have religious experiences of direct association with the deity. Such an occurrence would be called *mystical.*

off of Avoid using *of* in such sentences as "she walked *off of* the soccer field." Write "She walked *off* the soccer field."

precede, proceed   *Precede* means to go ahead of, as in a line: "Stephanie will *precede* Ralph in the graduation line." *Proceed* means simply to go ahead with an action: "We will now *proceed* with the conferring of the degrees."

presently, at present   *Presently* means soon, or shortly: "I will join you *presently.*" *At present* means now, currently, at this time: "*At present,* he is in his office."

principal, principle   *Principal* is usually an adjective: *principal cities, principal people.* It has become a noun in a few usages where the noun it formerly modified has been dropped. "He was the *principal* (teacher) of the school." "I withdrew the *principal* (amount) and interest from my savings account." "He acted as the *principal* (person) rather than as an agent." The noun *principle* means a basic law or doctrine: "The country was founded on the *principle* that all men are created equal."

raise, rise   *Raise* is a transitive verb: "*Raise* the flag." *Rise* (meaning *to get up, to ascend*) is intransitive: "The sun *rose* as usual."

rare, scarce   *Rare* and *scarce* refer to hard to find items that exist in small quantities. *Rare* usually implies exceptional quality or value: "If it is a really *rare* book, it will be quite expensive." *Scarce* can be applied to ordinary things, usually those that were previously abundant: "Potatoes are usually plentiful in the supermarket, but the drought has made them *scarce.*"

reason is because   The words *reason is* (*was,* etc.) should be followed by a statement of the reason: "The reason for his failure was illness." "The reason for the strict rules is to enforce discipline." Similar statements can be made by using *because:* "He failed because of illness." "The rules are strict because it is necessary to enforce discipline." *Reason* and *because* convey the same sense. It is illogical to use both words to convey the same meaning.

regardless, irregardless *Irregardless,* a nonstandard word, probably is patterned after *irrespective.* *Regardless,* which means without regard to or despite, is the correct form: "*Regardless* of his frank comments, I like him."

respectable, respectful *Respectable* means "worthy of respect or esteem," as in "She had a *respectable* command of the German language." *Respectful* means "showing respect for something else," as in "The teacher received the *respectful* attention of the class." Many letters are closed with "*Respectfully* yours."

rightfully, rightly *Rightful* or *rightfully* means having a just or legally established claim: "She was the *rightful* owner of the property." *Rightly* means properly or correctly, without the legal claim: "He *rightly* refused to comment."

same Do not use *same* as a pronoun: "I have your order for the books and will send *them* (NOT will send *same*)."

stationary, stationery *Stationary,* an adjective, means standing still or having a fixed position. *Stationery,* a noun, means writing materials, especially paper.

their, there, they're Be careful to distinguish the spelling of the possessive case of the pronoun *their* (*their books*) from the spelling of the adverb and the expletive *there*. and the contraction *they're*. "I got *there* before I knew it." "*There* are forty grapefruit in the crate." "*They're* waiting for us."

tortuous, torturous *Tortuous* means full of twists or bends: "The car was moving too fast for such a *tortuous*, crooked road." *Torturous* means inflicting great pain in a cruel manner: "The *torturous* devices were everywhere in the prison camps."

unique *Unique* means the only one of its kind: "His was a *unique* personality." It cannot logically be used in a comparative or superlative form. Something may be more or most odd, rare, unusual, peculiar. remarkable, etc., but NOT more or most unique.

who's, whose *Who's* is the contraction for *who is* and *who has:* "I cannot imagine *who's* coming." *Whose* is the possessive form of *who:* "We knew the family *whose* house was robbed."

woman, women Just as the plural of *man* is *men, so* the plural of *woman* is *women.*

you're, your *You're* is the contraction of *you are.* *Your* is the possessive form of the pronoun *you:* "*Your* birthday is tomorrow."

Chapter 9
Which Prepositions Go with Which Verbs?

Prepositions are necessary words because they show the spatial or temporal relationships between physical things. But one problem in using prepositions is choosing the appropriate one to go with certain verbs. Most of the time there is no problem, and we know what is meant when someone says, "He was with the car" or "He was in the car." But it is more difficult when we consider the subtle choice between "He spoke with anger" or "He spoke in anger."

In many cases, however, certain idiomatic combinations of verbs and prepositions have been firmly established in the language, and these should be respected. For example, we can say *agree to,* but not *agree at,* and *decide on,* but not *decide in.* More than likely, when a certain preposition sounds more familiar in a given context than another preposition, the more familiar one is the better. The following discussion of various prepositions includes many of the troublesome idiomatic combinations.

about   The preposition *about* sometimes means *around* or *circling,* as in "He walked *about* the town." It also sometimes means *approximately,* as in "She came *about* six o'clock." With a compound verb, the use of *about* weakens the sentence and makes it less precise: "I had forgotten that" is stronger than "I had forgotten *about* that."

at, in   These prepositions can sometimes be used interchangeably, with resulting slight differences in meaning. "The meeting was held *at* the church" and "The meeting was held *in* the church" mean virtually the same thing. "She is *at* the theater" suggests that she is a spectator at a play, but "She is *in* the theater" could indicate that she is in the building or that she is an actress in the profession of acting. The word *in* is used in reference to cities; normally we say, "He is *in* Boston," not "He is *at* Boston."

by   The preposition *by* usually means *near,* as in "He was standing *by* the pond." When used with time, it means *not later than,* as in "I'll be home *by* midnight." With verbs of motion, *by* can suggest *to avoid* or *to ignore,* as in "He walked right *by* her," or "Death passed her *by.*"

for   There are many meanings of the preposition *for.* It can be used to show distance, as in "Walk *for* a mile" or time, as in "Wait *for* a year." It can also indicate destination, as in "We set out *for* Hartford." It can even mean that we favor something or some-one, as in "We are *for* the mayor." Rarely does one have problems deciding which verbs to use with *for.*

in, into   Although *into* is sometimes used inter-changeably with *in,* it can also be used to intensify a meaning. "He looked *into* the report" is much stronger than "He looked *at* the report." In another combination, "consist *in*" refers to inherent quali-ties, as in "The value of education consists *in* its enlarging the ability to comprehend cultures different from our own." *Consist of* is used to refer to component parts of an entity, as in "A government consists *of* the legislative, judicial, and executive branches."

up, down   *Up* sometimes carries the meaning of completion, as in *fill up, hurry up, drink up* (but "drink it *down*"). In the cases of *burn down* and *burn up, down* and *up* are intensives, and either phrase means total destruction by fire, either by being leveled to the ground or by going up in smoke. *Burn down* is used only with structures, or perhaps with candles, but *burn up* can refer to anything, such as important papers, etc. One would never use an intensive in burning rubbish or other trivial things. There are also differences between *close up* and *close down.* Whereas one might innocuously *close up* the house for the night, to *close down* a gambling casino suggests that force is used. The phrases *load up* and *load down,* which have the same basic meaning, are used in American English in an unusual way. *Load up* is used in the active, as in "*Load up* on food before we go camping." *Load down* is used in the passive, as in "She was *loaded down* with cans of food."

with, to   The prepositions *with* and *to* have many possible uses as function words, and some of these uses may seem to overlap, leading to confusion. An object can be *similar to* or *identical with* another object. The phrase *according to* is idiomatic; *according with* is not. One can *conform to* or *conform with* the regulations. But be careful: "*in accordance with* the rules" is correct; "*in accordance to* them" is not.

Sentences calling for phrases such as *superior to* and *prior to* are sometimes written incorrectly and unidiomatically as *superior than* or *prior than.* Do not, however, disavow *than* entirely; its use is idiomatic in "I am *larger than* my brother" or "They are *poorer than* church mice."

Chapter 10
A Brief Glossary of Basic Grammatical Terms

abstract noun   An abstract noun designates intangibles, such as ideas like *liberty, love,* and *truth.*

active voice The active verb form indicates that the subject of a sentence is acting, not being acted upon: The lion *mauled* the hunter.

adjective   An adjective modifies (describes) nouns or pronouns: In the *hot* climate, he was always too *warm.*

adverb   An adverb modifies verbs, adjectives, and other adverbs: run *swiftly, very* pretty, *too warmly* dressed (*too*, an adverb, modified *warmly*, an adverb).

agreement   The subject and verb must *agree* in number. "They *go* to class at ten" is correct; "They *goes* to class at ten" is not.

article   A word like *the* or *a, an* signals that a noun will follow (also called a determiner).

case   Pronouns come in various forms, or *cases*, which indicate how the pronoun functions in a sentence. The nominative case (used as a subject) comes in forms such as *we, I, she*. The possessive case (used as an adjective) has such forms as *my* cap, *your* glove. The objective case, indicating the pronoun is being acted upon, takes such forms as *them, us, him.*

collective noun   A collective noun uses a singular form to indicate a group of individuals or things: *team, jury, congress.*

comparison   Comparison denotes the change in the forms of adjectives and adverbs to show degree. There are three forms of comparison: positive (*heavy, rapidly, good*); comparative (*heavier, more rapidly, better*); superlative (*heaviest, most rapidly, best*).

compound adjective   An adjective made up of two or more words: *run-of-the-mill, downcast.*

compound noun   A compound noun consists of more than one word, used as a unit: *fathers-in-law, booby trap, passersby, redhead.*

compound predicate   A compound predicate consists of two or more verbs functioning equally in a sentence: They *washed* and *waxed* the car.

compound sentence   A compound sentence contains at least two main clauses (independent clauses): I have always enjoyed reading novels, but my interest has recently turned to history and biography.

compound subject   A compound subject consists of two or more subjects functioning equally in a sentence: *Tom* and *Harry* had a great time at the game.

concrete noun   A concrete noun names things that are tangible, as opposed to abstract: *jewels, coins, eggs, dogs.*

conjugation   To conjugate is to list the forms of a verb showing tense, voice, mood, person, and number. For example, the conjugation of the verb *believe* in the present tense, active voice, indicative mood is *I believe, you believe, he/she/it believes, we believe, you believe, they believe.*

conjunction A conjunction links two parts of a sentence. *And, or, but, nor,* and *for* are coordinating conjunctions; *although, as if,* and *because* are subordinating conjunctions.

conjunctive adverb A conjunctive adverb joins two main clauses in a sentence: We hoped to take a ride in the country; *however,* our car would not start.

contractions Contractions are words that have been shortened. Apostrophes are used to indicate missing letters in such words as *she'll* and *don't.*

coordinate adjectives Coordinate adjectives consist of two or more adjectives that modify the same noun or pronoun: The *dark, damp* cave was spooky.

coordinating conjunction A coordinating conjunction (linking word) connects main clauses: It was cold and rainy, *and* the little boy was ready to go home.

definite article A definite article refers to a specific person, place, or thing: *the* doctor (not *a* doctor).

demonstrative pronoun A demonstrative pronoun points out objects without naming them: *These* are smaller than *those.*

dependent clause A dependent clause is subordinate to a main clause and cannot stand alone: *When the bell rang,* the class rushed out.

direct address In direct address a noun or pronoun, usually set off by commas, indicates the person or persons being spoken to: *Paula,* what happened to you? As you see, *ladies,* we have a problem.

direct object   The direct object is a word or word group that receives the action of a transitive verb, a verbal, or a preposition, as in the following: The punter kicked the *ball*. We sat watching the *people*. This treat is on *me*.

function word   A function word indicates the relationship between other words in a sentence. Function words can be articles (*the, a, an*), conjunctions (*and, but*), or prepositions (*for, of, in*).

future perfect tense   The future perfect is a verb form that indicate an action will be completed in the future prior to another future action: He *will have returned* before you leave on your trip.

future tense   The future tense is a verb form that indicates an action will take place later than the present; it is formed with the auxiliary *shall* or *will:* I *shall* eat spaghetti tonight.

gender   Nouns and pronouns are designated as masculine (*him, man*); feminine (*her, girl*); or neuter (*it, car*).

genitive case   The genitive case of a noun or pronoun indicates possession, as in *Bob's* book, the *General's* car, *his* book, and that is *hers*.

gerund   A gerund is a verbal that functions as a noun and has an *-ing* suffix: *Swimming* is good exercise. I like *flying*.

indefinite pronoun   An indefinite pronoun is one of a large group of words used as pronouns that do not express a definite number; examples include *all, everyone, nothing, somebody*.

independent clause An independent clause (also called a main clause or principal clause) can stand alone as a sentence: Although he was only a child, *Mozart understood musical theory.*

indirect object An indirect object acts as a noun and does not receive the action (as does a direct object) but indicates for or to whom something is done: I gave *Emily* the apple. (*Apple* is the direct object; *Emily* is the indirect object.)

intensifier An intensifier is a modifying word that makes the word it modifies more emphatic: *awfully, highly, very.*

interjections Interjections exclaim and command the reader or listener to give attention: *Wow! Hey! Say! Let's hear it for Oscar!*

interrogative An interrogative word or a statement has the force of a question: What? Do you really mean that?

intransitive verb An intransitive verb does not require an objective: The dog *died.* She *blushed* at the rude remark.

irregular verb An irregular verb does not form its past tenses and past participles by the addition of *d* or *ed: give, gave, given; go, went, gone.*

linking verb A linking verb relates a subject to its complement. The most common linking verbs are the forms of *to be:* She *is* kind. Linking verbs also relate to the senses: She looks *beautiful. Become* and *seems* are also common linking verbs: He *seems* sad. Adjectives, not adverbs, follow linking verbs. Just as you would not say "She looks *beautifully*," you would not say "She feels *badly.*"

mass nouns   Mass nouns name things not normally counted, such as *water, grain, rice.*

mood   Mood is the form of a verb that indicates the condition or nature of the expression. The *indicative* mood is used when making statements or asking questions: He is ready. Are you ready? The *imperative* mood is used when giving commands: Be ready! The *subjunctive* mood is used when expressing a wish or a condition contrary to fact: I wish I were King. If I were you, I would go. (Note that *was* would be incorrect in both these sentences.)

nominative case, of pronouns   The nominative case indicates that a pronoun is to be used as the subject of a verb or subject complement: *I, he, she, they, it.*

nonrestrictive modifier   A nonrestrictive modifier is a phrase or clause that modifies terms but does not limit or identify them. Nonrestrictive elements are always set off by commas: This low-priced airfare, *valid for only this month*, is a real bargain. Food, *which we all must have*, is both necessary and pleasure-giving.

nonstandard language   Nonstandard language does not conform in idiom, choice of words, grammar, or pronunciation to usage generally accepted by educated speakers of the language: *ain't, don't never, alright.*

nouns   Nouns name persons, places, things, or ideas: *arrow, Jonathan, Philadelphia, democracy.* The plural of most nouns in formed by adding *s* (*horses, cows*) or by adding *es* (*foxes, boxes*); some words of Latin origin form plurals in other ways: *radius, radii* (also *radiuses*); *stadium, stadia.*

number   The number of a verb, noun, pronoun, or demonstrative adverb indicate whether it is singular or plural: *man, men; he, she, they; this, these; goes, go.*

objective case   The objective case of a noun or pronoun indicates the word is functioning as the object of a verb, verbal, or preposition: We defeated *them.* He included *me* in the program.

participle   A participle is a verbal used as an adjective. Present participles end in *-ing,* as in *running, smiling.* Past participles end in *d, ed, t, n, en,* as in *eaten, finished:* The *smiling* carpenter admired the *finished* product.

passive voice   The passive voice is a verb form that indicates the subject is being acted upon: The flower pots *were brought* indoors out of the cold. The pie *was eaten* with gusto.

past perfect tense   The past perfect tense of a verb indicates an action occurred in the past: She *had gone* before Enrico returned.

past tense   The past tense of a verb indicates an action occurred in the past: She *spoke* softly. He *left* quietly.

perfect tense   The perfect tense of a verb is used with *have* or *had* to indicate a completed action: I *have read* it. (present perfect) I *had read* it. (past perfect) I *will have read* it. (future perfect)

phrase   A phrase is a group of words that are related but that lack a subject or predicate (or both): *a pack of lies, a piece of cake.*

possessive case   The possessive case of a noun or pronoun indicates ownership: *Jerry's* dog, the *teacher's* chalk; *his* dog, the chalk is *hers.*

predicate   The predicate of a sentence contains a single verb or compound verbs: She *ran* a good race. Jack *fell* down and *broke* his crown.

preposition   A preposition links pronouns and nouns to the rest of the sentence: *in, after, over, between, under, at, for, about, beside, from, within.*

prepositional phrase   A prepositional phrase contains a preposition, its object, and any modifiers. It can function in the sentence as an adjective, adverb, or noun: *in the deep jungle, of uncertain origin, out of business.*

present participle   A present participle is a verbal that indicates continuing action: My head is *reeling*. I like to watch the *passing* crowds from a sidewalk café.

present perfect tense   The present perfect tense of a verb refers to a single action already completed: I *have read* it. You *have seen* the movie.

present tense   The present tense of a verb indicates the action is occurring in the present. I *jog*. You *run*.

principal parts of verbs   There are three verb forms from which the various tenses are formed: infinitive, or plain form (*sit, stand*); past tense (*sat, stood*); past participle (*have sat, have stood*).

pronoun   A pronoun is used in place of a noun or noun phrase: *I, it, she* (personal pronouns); *myself, herself* (reflexive pronouns); *this, that* (demonstrative pronouns).

regular verb   A regular verb forms its past tense and past participle by adding *d* or *ed* to the plain infinitive form of the verb.

subjective case   The subjective case of a noun or pronoun indicates the word functions as the subject of a sentence; also called the *nominative* case: *I* am unhappy. *She* is joyful.

subjunctive mood The subjunctive form of a verb indicates the speaker is expressing a wish, a condition contrary to fact, a recommendation, or a request: I wish I *were* King. If I *were* King, I would rule justly. Would you recommend that I *be* King?

subordinate clause A subordinate clause is dependent on the main clause in a sentence: *After I finish studying*, I will watch television.

subordinating conjunction A subordinating conjunction (*as, because, although*) joins sentence elements of unequal importance: He had to walk *because* the car would not start.

transitive verb A transitive verb conveys action and takes an object: He *tells* lies. She *earns* money.

verb A verb is a word or group of words that indicates what state of being the subject is in or what the subject is doing: *is, are, was, lie, lay, fall, fell.*

verbal Verbals are verb forms used as nouns, adjectives, or adverbs: *Relaxing* is important (gerund). The *brewed* tea is best (participle). The coffee was too hot *to drink* (infinitive).

Chapter 11
Conjugations and Principal Parts

Conjugation of the Verb *To Be*

Infinitive: to be, be
Perfect Infinitive: to have been
Present Participle: being
Present Perfect Participle: having been
Past Participle: been

INDICATIVE MOOD

Person	Singular	Plural
	PRESENT TENSE	
First	I am	we are
Second	you are	you are
Third	he (she, it) is	they are
	FUTURE TENSE	
First	I shall be	we shall be
Second	you will be	you will be
Third	he (she, it) will be	they will be
	PAST TENSE	
First	I was	we were
Second	you were	you were
Third	he (she, it) was	they were
	PRESENT PERFECT TENSE	
First	I have been	we have been
Second	you have been	you have been

Person	Singular	Plural
Third	he (she, it) has been	they have been

PAST PERFECT TENSE

First	I had been	we had been
Second	you had been	you had been
Third	he (she, it) had been	they had been

FUTURE PERFECT TENSE

First	I shall have been	we shall have been
Second	you will have been	you will have been
Third	he (she, it) will have been	they will have been

IMPERATIVE MOOD

be

SUBJUNCTIVE MOOD

Present Tense: if I (you, he, she, it, we, they) be
Past Tense: if I (you, he, she, it, we, they) were

Conjugation of the Verb *To Drive*

ACTIVE VOICE	PASSIVE VOICE
Infinitive: to drive, drive	to be driven, be driven
Perfect Infinitive: to have driven	to have been driven
Present Participle: driving	being driven
Perfect Participle: having driven	having been driven
Past Participle: driven	had been driven

INDICATIVE MOOD

Singular	Plural

PRESENT TENSE

1. I drive   we drive
   I am driven   we are driven

2. you drive   you drive
   you are driven   you are driven

3. he (she, it) drives   they drive
   he (she, it) is driven   they are driven

FUTURE TENSE

1. I shall drive   we shall drive
   I shall be driven   we shall be driven

2. you will drive   you will drive
   you will be driven   you will be driven

3. he will drive   they will drive
   he will be driven   they will be driven

PAST TENSE

1. I drove   we drove
   I was driven   we were driven

2. you drove   you drove
   you were driven   you were driven

3. he drove   they drove
   he was driven   they were driven

PRESENT PERFECT TENSE

1. I have driven   we have driven
   I have been driven   we have been driven

Singular	Plural
2. you have driven	you have driven
you have been driven	you have been driven
3. he has driven	they have driven
he has been driven	they have been driven

PAST PERFECT TENSE

1. I had driven	we had driven
I had been driven	we had been driven
2. you had driven	you had driven
you had been driven	you had been driven
3. he had driven	they had driven
he had been driven	they had been driven

FUTURE PERFECT TENSE

1. shall have driven	we shall have driven
I shall have been driven	we shall have been driven
2. you will have driven	you will have driven
you will have been driven	you will have been driven
3. he will have driven	they will have driven
he will have been driven	they will have been driven

IMPERATIVE MOOD

drive

SUBJUNCTIVE MOOD

PRESENT TENSE

if I (you, he, she, it, we, they) drive

if I (you, he, she, it, we, they) be driven

PAST TENSE

if I (you, he, she, it, we, they) drove

if I (you, he, she, it, we, they) were driven

Principal Parts of Irregular Verbs

Regular verbs form the past tense and past participle by adding *-ed* (*discover—discovered, cry—cried*) or *-d* (*raise—raised, tie—tied*) to the infinitive. Verbs that do not follow these principles are known as irregular verbs. The following is a list of the principal parts of the most frequently used irregular verbs.

Infinitive and Present Tense	Past Tense	Past Participle
arise	arose	arisen
awake	awoke, awaked	awaked, awoke, awoken
bear	bore	borne (born— passive voice)
beat	beat	beaten, beat
begin	began	begun
bend	bent	bent
bid (offer)	bid	bid
bid (command)	bade	bidden
bind	bound	bound
bite	bit	bitten, bit
blow	blew	blown

Infinitive and Present Tense	Past Tense	Past Participle
break	broke	broken
bring	brought	brought
broadcast	broadcast, broadcasted	broadcast, broadcasted
build	built	built
burst	burst	burst
buy	bought	bought
cast	cast	cast
catch	caught	caught
choose	chose	chosen
cling	clung	clung
come	came	come
creep	crept	crept
deal	dealt	dealt
dive	dived, dove	dived
do	did	done
draw	drew	drawn
drink	drank	drunk
drive	drove	driven
eat	ate	eaten
fall	fell	fallen
feed	fed	fed
feel	felt	felt
fight	fought	fought
find	found	found
flee	fled	fled
fling	flung	flung
fly	flew	flown
forbear	forbore	forborne
forbid	forbade, forbad	forbidden
forget	forgot	forgotten, forgot

Infinitive and Present Tense	Past Tense	Past Participle
forgive	forgave	forgiven
forsake	forsook	forsaken
freeze	froze	frozen
get	got	got, gotten
give	gave	given
go	went	gone
grow	grew	grown
hang	hung (hanged—executed)	hung (hanged—executed)
have (has)	had	had
hit	hit	hit
hold	held	held
hurt	hurt	hurt
kneel	knelt, kneeled	knelt
know	knew	known
lead	led	led
leap	leaped, leapt	leaped, leapt
leave	left	left
lend	lent	lent
let	let	let
lie	lay	lain
lose	lost	lost
make	made	made
meet	met	met
put	put	put
read	read	read
rend	rent	rent
ride	rode	ridden
ring	rang	rung
rise	rose	risen
run	ran	run

Infinitive and Present Tense	Past Tense	Past Participle
see	saw	seen
seek	sought	sought
sell	sold	sold
send	sent	sent
set	set	set
shine	shone	shone
shrink	shrank, shrunk	shrunk, shrunken
sing	sang	sung
sink	sank	sunk
slay	slew	slain
sit	sat	sat
sleep	slept	slept
slide	slid	slid
sling	slung	slung
slink	slunk	slunk
speak	spoke	spoken
spring	sprang, sprung	sprung
steal	stole	stolen
stick	stuck	stuck
sting	stung	stung
stride	strode	stridden
strike	struck	struck
swear	swore	sworn
sweat	sweat, sweated	sweated
sweep	swept	swept
swim	swam	swum
swing	swung	swung
take	took	taken
teach	taught	taught
tear	tore	torn
tell	told	told

Infinitive and Present Tense	Past Tense	Past Participle
think	thought	thought
thrive	throve, thrived	thrived, thriven
throw	threw	thrown
wake	waked, woke	waked, woken, woke
wear	wore	worn
weep	wept	wept
win	won	won
wind	wound	wound
work	worked, wrought	worked, wrought
wring	wrung	wrung
write	wrote	written